50 Vegan Classic Recipes for Home

By: Kelly Johnson

Table of Contents

- Vegan lasagna
- Chickpea curry
- Vegan mac and cheese
- Lentil soup
- Tofu stir-fry
- Vegetable curry
- Quinoa salad
- Vegan chili
- Mushroom risotto
- Black bean tacos
- Stuffed bell peppers
- Vegan shepherd's pie
- Eggplant parmesan
- Vegan pad thai
- Ratatouille
- Lentil shepherd's pie
- Vegan stuffed shells
- Veggie burgers
- Vegan spaghetti carbonara
- Cauliflower buffalo wings
- Vegan sushi rolls
- Butternut squash soup
- Sweet potato casserole
- Vegan mushroom stroganoff
- Lentil meatballs
- Vegan BBQ pulled jackfruit
- Vegan jambalaya
- Vegan gnocchi
- Vegan meatloaf
- Chickpea salad sandwiches
- Vegan pesto pasta
- Jackfruit tacos
- Vegan moussaka
- Vegan paella
- Vegan sloppy joes

- Vegan pot pie
- Vegan coconut curry
- Vegan spinach and artichoke dip
- Vegan stuffed cabbage rolls
- Vegan falafel
- Vegan mushroom gravy
- Vegan risotto
- Vegan broccoli cheddar soup
- Vegan quiche
- Vegan tofu scramble
- Vegan cashew cheese sauce
- Vegan mushroom bourguignon
- Vegan pumpkin soup
- Vegan tempeh bacon
- Vegan chocolate avocado mousse

Vegan lasagna

Ingredients:

For the lasagna noodles:

- 12 lasagna noodles (regular or gluten-free)

For the tofu ricotta:

- 1 block (14-16 ounces) firm tofu, drained and pressed
- 2 tablespoons nutritional yeast
- 1 tablespoon lemon juice
- 1 teaspoon garlic powder
- 1 teaspoon onion powder
- 1/2 teaspoon dried basil
- 1/2 teaspoon dried oregano
- Salt and black pepper, to taste

For the marinara sauce:

- 2 tablespoons olive oil
- 1 onion, chopped
- 3 cloves garlic, minced
- 1 can (28 ounces) crushed tomatoes
- 1 can (14 ounces) diced tomatoes
- 2 teaspoons dried basil
- 1 teaspoon dried oregano
- Salt and black pepper, to taste

For the vegan cheese sauce:

- 1 cup raw cashews, soaked in hot water for 1 hour
- 1 cup unsweetened non-dairy milk (such as almond milk or soy milk)

- 1/4 cup nutritional yeast
- 1 tablespoon lemon juice
- 1 teaspoon garlic powder
- 1/2 teaspoon onion powder
- Salt and black pepper, to taste

Instructions:

1. Preheat your oven to 375°F (190°C). Grease a 9x13-inch baking dish with olive oil or cooking spray.
2. Cook the lasagna noodles according to the package instructions until al dente. Drain the cooked noodles and set them aside.
3. To make the tofu ricotta, crumble the drained and pressed tofu into a mixing bowl. Add the nutritional yeast, lemon juice, garlic powder, onion powder, dried basil, dried oregano, salt, and black pepper. Mix until well combined and the mixture resembles ricotta cheese. Set aside.
4. To make the marinara sauce, heat the olive oil in a large skillet over medium heat. Add the chopped onion and minced garlic, and sauté until softened and fragrant, about 5-7 minutes.
5. Stir in the crushed tomatoes, diced tomatoes, dried basil, dried oregano, salt, and black pepper. Simmer the sauce for 10-15 minutes, stirring occasionally, to allow the flavors to meld together.
6. To make the vegan cheese sauce, drain the soaked cashews and place them in a blender. Add the non-dairy milk, nutritional yeast, lemon juice, garlic powder, onion powder, salt, and black pepper. Blend until smooth and creamy, adding more non-dairy milk as needed to reach your desired consistency.
7. To assemble the lasagna, spread a thin layer of marinara sauce on the bottom of the prepared baking dish. Arrange a layer of cooked lasagna noodles on top of the sauce.
8. Spread half of the tofu ricotta mixture evenly over the noodles, followed by a layer of marinara sauce and a drizzle of vegan cheese sauce.
9. Repeat the layers with the remaining noodles, tofu ricotta, marinara sauce, and vegan cheese sauce, finishing with a layer of vegan cheese sauce on top.
10. Cover the baking dish with aluminum foil and bake the lasagna in the preheated oven for 30 minutes.
11. Remove the foil and bake the lasagna for an additional 15-20 minutes, or until the top is golden brown and bubbly.

12. Once baked, remove the vegan lasagna from the oven and let it cool for a few minutes before slicing and serving.
13. Garnish the slices of vegan lasagna with fresh basil or parsley, if desired.
14. Enjoy your homemade vegan lasagna as a delicious and satisfying plant-based meal!

Chickpea curry

Ingredients:

- 2 tablespoons coconut oil or vegetable oil
- 1 onion, finely chopped
- 3 cloves garlic, minced
- 1 tablespoon fresh ginger, grated
- 1 tablespoon curry powder
- 1 teaspoon ground cumin
- 1 teaspoon ground coriander
- 1/2 teaspoon ground turmeric
- 1/4 teaspoon cayenne pepper (optional, for extra heat)
- 1 can (14 ounces) diced tomatoes
- 2 cans (15 ounces each) chickpeas, drained and rinsed
- 1 can (13.5 ounces) coconut milk
- Salt and black pepper, to taste
- Fresh cilantro, for garnish
- Cooked rice or naan bread, for serving

Instructions:

1. Heat the coconut oil or vegetable oil in a large skillet or pot over medium heat.
2. Add the chopped onion to the skillet and sauté until softened and translucent, about 5 minutes.
3. Stir in the minced garlic and grated ginger, and cook for an additional 1-2 minutes, until fragrant.
4. Add the curry powder, ground cumin, ground coriander, ground turmeric, and cayenne pepper (if using) to the skillet. Stir well to coat the onions and spices.
5. Pour in the diced tomatoes (with their juices) and chickpeas, stirring to combine with the onion and spice mixture.
6. Pour in the coconut milk and stir to combine. Bring the mixture to a simmer.
7. Reduce the heat to low and let the chickpea curry simmer gently for 15-20 minutes, stirring occasionally, until the flavors have melded together and the curry has thickened slightly.
8. Taste the chickpea curry and adjust the seasoning with salt and black pepper, as needed.
9. Once cooked, remove the chickpea curry from the heat.

10. Serve the chickpea curry hot, garnished with fresh cilantro, alongside cooked rice or naan bread.
11. Enjoy your homemade chickpea curry as a delicious and satisfying plant-based meal!

Feel free to customize the chickpea curry recipe by adding other vegetables such as spinach, bell peppers, or potatoes for extra flavor and nutrition. You can also adjust the level of spiciness by adding more or less cayenne pepper according to your taste preferences.

Vegan mac and cheese

Ingredients:

- 12 ounces (about 340g) elbow macaroni or your favorite pasta shape (use gluten-free pasta if needed)
- 2 cups peeled and diced potatoes
- 1 cup peeled and diced carrots
- 1/2 cup raw cashews, soaked in hot water for 1 hour or overnight
- 1/4 cup nutritional yeast
- 1/4 cup refined coconut oil or vegan butter
- 1/4 cup unsweetened non-dairy milk (such as almond milk or soy milk)
- 2 tablespoons lemon juice
- 1 teaspoon garlic powder
- 1 teaspoon onion powder
- 1/2 teaspoon smoked paprika
- Salt and black pepper, to taste
- Chopped fresh parsley, for garnish (optional)

Instructions:

1. Cook the elbow macaroni or pasta according to the package instructions until al dente. Drain the cooked pasta and set it aside.
2. In a medium saucepan, add the diced potatoes and carrots. Cover them with water and bring the water to a boil. Cook the vegetables until they are fork-tender, about 10-15 minutes.
3. While the potatoes and carrots are cooking, drain the soaked cashews and add them to a blender along with the nutritional yeast, refined coconut oil or vegan butter, non-dairy milk, lemon juice, garlic powder, onion powder, smoked paprika, salt, and black pepper.
4. Once the potatoes and carrots are cooked, drain them and add them to the blender with the cashew mixture.
5. Blend the mixture until smooth and creamy, scraping down the sides of the blender as needed to ensure everything is well combined.
6. Taste the sauce and adjust the seasoning with salt and black pepper, if needed.
7. Pour the creamy vegan cheese sauce over the cooked pasta in a large mixing bowl. Stir well to coat the pasta evenly with the sauce.

8. Transfer the coated pasta to a serving dish or individual bowls.
9. Garnish the vegan mac and cheese with chopped fresh parsley, if desired.
10. Serve the vegan mac and cheese hot as a comforting and delicious dairy-free meal!

Feel free to customize the vegan mac and cheese recipe by adding other ingredients such as roasted garlic, diced tomatoes, sautéed mushrooms, or chopped spinach for extra flavor and texture variations. You can also bake the mac and cheese in the oven with a breadcrumb topping for a crispy finish.

Lentil soup

Ingredients:

- 1 tablespoon olive oil
- 1 onion, chopped
- 2 carrots, diced
- 2 celery stalks, diced
- 3 cloves garlic, minced
- 1 cup dried lentils (green or brown), rinsed and picked over
- 4 cups vegetable broth or water
- 1 can (14 ounces) diced tomatoes
- 1 teaspoon ground cumin
- 1 teaspoon ground coriander
- 1/2 teaspoon smoked paprika
- 1/2 teaspoon dried thyme
- Salt and black pepper, to taste
- Juice of 1 lemon
- Chopped fresh parsley or cilantro, for garnish (optional)

Instructions:

1. In a large pot or Dutch oven, heat the olive oil over medium heat. Add the chopped onion, diced carrots, and diced celery. Sauté the vegetables until they are softened, about 5-7 minutes.
2. Add the minced garlic to the pot and cook for an additional 1-2 minutes, until fragrant.
3. Stir in the dried lentils, vegetable broth or water, diced tomatoes (with their juices), ground cumin, ground coriander, smoked paprika, and dried thyme. Season the soup with salt and black pepper, to taste.
4. Bring the soup to a boil, then reduce the heat to low and let it simmer, partially covered, for 25-30 minutes, or until the lentils are tender.
5. Once the lentils are cooked, remove the pot from the heat. Use an immersion blender to blend the soup until smooth and creamy, or blend half of the soup in a blender and return it to the pot.
6. Stir in the lemon juice, adjusting the amount to taste.

7. Taste the lentil soup and adjust the seasoning with salt and black pepper, if needed.
8. Ladle the lentil soup into bowls and garnish with chopped fresh parsley or cilantro, if desired.
9. Serve the lentil soup hot as a comforting and nutritious meal!

Feel free to customize the lentil soup recipe by adding other vegetables such as spinach, kale, or diced potatoes for extra flavor and nutrition. You can also add spices like turmeric, curry powder, or chili flakes for additional depth of flavor.

Tofu stir-fry

Ingredients:

For the tofu:

- 1 block (14-16 ounces) firm tofu
- 2 tablespoons soy sauce or tamari
- 1 tablespoon cornstarch
- 1 tablespoon vegetable oil

For the stir-fry:

- 2 tablespoons vegetable oil
- 1 onion, sliced
- 2 bell peppers, sliced (any color)
- 1 cup broccoli florets
- 1 carrot, sliced
- 2 cloves garlic, minced
- 1 tablespoon fresh ginger, grated
- 1/4 cup soy sauce or tamari
- 2 tablespoons rice vinegar
- 1 tablespoon maple syrup or brown sugar
- 1 tablespoon cornstarch dissolved in 2 tablespoons water
- Cooked rice or noodles, for serving
- Sesame seeds or chopped green onions, for garnish (optional)

Instructions:

1. Start by preparing the tofu. Drain the tofu and pat it dry with paper towels to remove excess moisture. Cut the tofu into cubes or strips.
2. In a small bowl, whisk together the soy sauce or tamari and cornstarch until smooth. Add the tofu to the bowl and toss to coat evenly.
3. Heat the vegetable oil in a large skillet or wok over medium-high heat. Add the tofu in a single layer and cook until golden brown and crispy on all sides, about 5-7 minutes. Remove the tofu from the skillet and set it aside.

4. In the same skillet or wok, heat the remaining vegetable oil over medium-high heat. Add the sliced onion, bell peppers, broccoli florets, and carrot. Stir-fry the vegetables until they are tender-crisp, about 5-7 minutes.
5. Add the minced garlic and grated ginger to the skillet and cook for an additional 1-2 minutes, until fragrant.
6. In a small bowl, whisk together the soy sauce or tamari, rice vinegar, and maple syrup or brown sugar. Pour the sauce over the vegetables in the skillet and stir to coat evenly.
7. Return the cooked tofu to the skillet and toss everything together until heated through.
8. Stir in the cornstarch-water mixture and cook for 1-2 minutes, until the sauce has thickened slightly.
9. Remove the skillet from the heat.
10. Serve the tofu stir-fry hot over cooked rice or noodles.
11. Garnish with sesame seeds or chopped green onions, if desired.
12. Enjoy your homemade tofu stir-fry as a delicious and satisfying meal!

Feel free to customize the tofu stir-fry recipe by adding other vegetables such as mushrooms, snap peas, or bok choy. You can also adjust the sauce to your taste by adding more or less soy sauce, rice vinegar, or maple syrup.

Vegetable curry

Ingredients:

- 2 tablespoons vegetable oil
- 1 onion, chopped
- 3 cloves garlic, minced
- 1 tablespoon fresh ginger, grated
- 2 tablespoons curry powder
- 1 teaspoon ground turmeric
- 1 teaspoon ground cumin
- 1 teaspoon ground coriander
- 1/2 teaspoon cayenne pepper (adjust to taste)
- 1 can (14 ounces) diced tomatoes
- 1 can (14 ounces) coconut milk
- 4 cups mixed vegetables (such as carrots, bell peppers, potatoes, cauliflower, peas, and green beans), chopped
- Salt and black pepper, to taste
- Cooked rice or naan bread, for serving
- Fresh cilantro, for garnish (optional)
- Lime wedges, for serving (optional)

Instructions:

1. Heat the vegetable oil in a large skillet or pot over medium heat.
2. Add the chopped onion to the skillet and sauté until softened and translucent, about 5 minutes.
3. Stir in the minced garlic and grated ginger, and cook for an additional 1-2 minutes, until fragrant.
4. Add the curry powder, ground turmeric, ground cumin, ground coriander, and cayenne pepper (if using) to the skillet. Stir well to coat the onions and spices.
5. Pour in the diced tomatoes (with their juices) and coconut milk, stirring to combine.
6. Add the chopped mixed vegetables to the skillet and stir to coat them with the curry sauce.
7. Bring the curry to a simmer, then reduce the heat to low and let it simmer gently for 15-20 minutes, or until the vegetables are tender.

8. Taste the vegetable curry and adjust the seasoning with salt and black pepper, if needed.
9. Once cooked, remove the vegetable curry from the heat.
10. Serve the vegetable curry hot over cooked rice or with naan bread on the side.
11. Garnish the vegetable curry with fresh cilantro and serve with lime wedges, if desired.
12. Enjoy your homemade vegetable curry as a flavorful and nutritious meal!

Feel free to customize the vegetable curry recipe by adding other ingredients such as chickpeas, lentils, tofu, or spinach for extra protein and texture. You can also adjust the level of spiciness by adding more or less cayenne pepper according to your taste preferences.

Vegetable curry

Ingredients:

- 2 tablespoons vegetable oil
- 1 onion, finely chopped
- 3 cloves garlic, minced
- 1 tablespoon fresh ginger, grated
- 2 tablespoons curry powder
- 1 teaspoon ground turmeric
- 1 teaspoon ground cumin
- 1 teaspoon ground coriander
- 1/2 teaspoon cayenne pepper (adjust to taste)
- 1 can (14 ounces) diced tomatoes
- 1 can (14 ounces) coconut milk
- 3 cups mixed vegetables (such as carrots, bell peppers, potatoes, cauliflower, peas, and green beans), chopped
- Salt, to taste
- Cooked rice or naan bread, for serving
- Fresh cilantro, for garnish (optional)
- Lime wedges, for serving (optional)

Instructions:

1. Heat the vegetable oil in a large skillet or pot over medium heat.
2. Add the chopped onion to the skillet and sauté until softened and translucent, about 5 minutes.
3. Stir in the minced garlic and grated ginger, and cook for an additional 1-2 minutes, until fragrant.
4. Add the curry powder, ground turmeric, ground cumin, ground coriander, and cayenne pepper (if using) to the skillet. Stir well to coat the onions and spices.
5. Pour in the diced tomatoes (with their juices) and coconut milk, stirring to combine.
6. Add the chopped mixed vegetables to the skillet and stir to coat them with the curry sauce.
7. Bring the curry to a simmer, then reduce the heat to low and let it simmer gently for 15-20 minutes, or until the vegetables are tender.

8. Taste the vegetable curry and adjust the seasoning with salt, if needed.
9. Once cooked, remove the vegetable curry from the heat.
10. Serve the vegetable curry hot over cooked rice or with naan bread on the side.
11. Garnish the vegetable curry with fresh cilantro and serve with lime wedges, if desired.
12. Enjoy your homemade vegetable curry as a flavorful and nutritious meal!

Feel free to customize the vegetable curry recipe by adding other ingredients such as chickpeas, lentils, tofu, or spinach for extra protein and texture. You can also adjust the level of spiciness by adding more or less cayenne pepper according to your taste preferences.

Quinoa salad

Ingredients:

- 1 cup quinoa, rinsed
- 2 cups water or vegetable broth
- 1 cucumber, diced
- 1 bell pepper, diced (any color)
- 1 cup cherry tomatoes, halved
- 1/4 cup red onion, finely chopped
- 1/4 cup fresh parsley, chopped
- 1/4 cup fresh mint, chopped
- 1/4 cup kalamata olives, sliced (optional)
- 1/4 cup crumbled feta cheese or vegan feta (optional)
- Juice of 1 lemon
- 2 tablespoons extra virgin olive oil
- 1 clove garlic, minced
- Salt and black pepper, to taste

Instructions:

1. In a medium saucepan, combine the quinoa and water or vegetable broth. Bring the mixture to a boil over medium-high heat.
2. Reduce the heat to low, cover, and simmer for 15-20 minutes, or until the quinoa is cooked and the liquid is absorbed. Remove the saucepan from the heat and let it sit, covered, for 5 minutes. Then fluff the quinoa with a fork and let it cool to room temperature.
3. In a large mixing bowl, combine the cooked quinoa, diced cucumber, diced bell pepper, halved cherry tomatoes, finely chopped red onion, chopped fresh parsley, chopped fresh mint, and sliced kalamata olives (if using).
4. In a small bowl, whisk together the lemon juice, extra virgin olive oil, minced garlic, salt, and black pepper to make the dressing.
5. Pour the dressing over the quinoa salad and toss to coat everything evenly.
6. If using, sprinkle the crumbled feta cheese or vegan feta over the quinoa salad and gently toss to combine.
7. Taste the quinoa salad and adjust the seasoning with salt and black pepper, if needed.

8. Serve the quinoa salad immediately, or cover and refrigerate for at least 1 hour to allow the flavors to meld together.
9. Enjoy your homemade quinoa salad as a delicious and nutritious meal or side dish!

Feel free to customize the quinoa salad recipe by adding other ingredients such as diced avocado, shredded carrots, chopped spinach, or cooked chickpeas for extra flavor and texture. You can also swap the herbs and add your favorite dressing for variety.

Vegan chili

Ingredients:

- 1 tablespoon olive oil
- 1 onion, chopped
- 3 cloves garlic, minced
- 1 bell pepper, diced (any color)
- 2 carrots, diced
- 2 celery stalks, diced
- 1 can (14 ounces) diced tomatoes
- 1 can (15 ounces) kidney beans, drained and rinsed
- 1 can (15 ounces) black beans, drained and rinsed
- 1 can (15 ounces) chickpeas, drained and rinsed
- 2 cups vegetable broth
- 1 tablespoon chili powder
- 1 teaspoon ground cumin
- 1 teaspoon smoked paprika
- 1/2 teaspoon dried oregano
- 1/2 teaspoon dried basil
- Salt and black pepper, to taste
- Optional toppings: diced avocado, chopped fresh cilantro, sliced green onions, vegan sour cream, or shredded vegan cheese

Instructions:

1. Heat the olive oil in a large pot over medium heat.
2. Add the chopped onion to the pot and sauté until softened and translucent, about 5 minutes.
3. Stir in the minced garlic and cook for an additional 1-2 minutes, until fragrant.
4. Add the diced bell pepper, diced carrots, and diced celery to the pot. Cook for 5-7 minutes, or until the vegetables are tender.
5. Stir in the diced tomatoes (with their juices), kidney beans, black beans, chickpeas, vegetable broth, chili powder, ground cumin, smoked paprika, dried oregano, and dried basil.
6. Season the chili with salt and black pepper, to taste.

7. Bring the chili to a simmer, then reduce the heat to low and let it simmer for 20-30 minutes, stirring occasionally, to allow the flavors to meld together and the chili to thicken.
8. Taste the chili and adjust the seasoning with salt and black pepper, if needed.
9. Once cooked, remove the chili from the heat.
10. Serve the vegan chili hot, topped with your favorite toppings such as diced avocado, chopped fresh cilantro, sliced green onions, vegan sour cream, or shredded vegan cheese.
11. Enjoy your homemade vegan chili as a delicious and satisfying meal!

Feel free to customize the vegan chili recipe by adding other ingredients such as diced tomatoes with green chilies for extra heat, corn kernels for sweetness, or diced potatoes for additional texture. You can also adjust the level of spiciness by adding more or less chili powder according to your taste preferences.

Mushroom risotto

Ingredients:

- 4 cups vegetable broth
- 2 tablespoons olive oil
- 1 onion, finely chopped
- 2 cloves garlic, minced
- 8 ounces mushrooms (such as cremini, button, or shiitake), sliced
- 1 1/2 cups Arborio rice
- 1/2 cup dry white wine (optional)
- 1/2 cup grated Parmesan cheese or nutritional yeast (for vegan option)
- Salt and black pepper, to taste
- Chopped fresh parsley, for garnish (optional)

Instructions:

1. In a medium saucepan, heat the vegetable broth over low heat. Keep it warm while you prepare the risotto.
2. In a large skillet or Dutch oven, heat the olive oil over medium heat.
3. Add the finely chopped onion to the skillet and sauté until softened and translucent, about 5 minutes.
4. Stir in the minced garlic and cook for an additional 1-2 minutes, until fragrant.
5. Add the sliced mushrooms to the skillet and cook until they are tender and golden brown, about 5-7 minutes.
6. Stir in the Arborio rice and cook for 1-2 minutes, stirring constantly, until the rice is lightly toasted.
7. If using, pour in the dry white wine and cook, stirring constantly, until the wine is absorbed by the rice.
8. Begin adding the warm vegetable broth to the skillet, one ladleful at a time, stirring frequently and allowing each addition of broth to be absorbed before adding more. Continue this process until the rice is creamy and tender, but still slightly al dente, about 20-25 minutes.
9. Once the risotto is cooked to your desired consistency, stir in the grated Parmesan cheese or nutritional yeast (for vegan option). Season with salt and black pepper, to taste.
10. Remove the skillet from the heat.

11. Serve the mushroom risotto hot, garnished with chopped fresh parsley, if desired.
12. Enjoy your homemade mushroom risotto as a delicious and satisfying meal!

Feel free to customize the mushroom risotto recipe by adding other ingredients such as chopped spinach, sun-dried tomatoes, or roasted garlic for extra flavor and texture. You can also experiment with different types of mushrooms for variety, or use vegetable broth infused with dried mushrooms for a richer flavor.

Black bean tacos

Ingredients:

For the black beans:

- 2 tablespoons olive oil
- 1 onion, finely chopped
- 2 cloves garlic, minced
- 2 cans (15 ounces each) black beans, drained and rinsed
- 1 teaspoon ground cumin
- 1 teaspoon chili powder
- 1/2 teaspoon smoked paprika
- Salt and black pepper, to taste
- Juice of 1 lime
- 2 tablespoons chopped fresh cilantro

For serving:

- 8 small corn or flour tortillas
- Toppings of your choice: shredded lettuce, diced tomatoes, diced avocado, sliced jalapeños, chopped cilantro, vegan sour cream, salsa, lime wedges, etc.

Instructions:

1. Heat the olive oil in a large skillet over medium heat.
2. Add the finely chopped onion to the skillet and sauté until softened and translucent, about 5 minutes.
3. Stir in the minced garlic and cook for an additional 1-2 minutes, until fragrant.
4. Add the drained and rinsed black beans to the skillet, along with the ground cumin, chili powder, smoked paprika, salt, and black pepper. Stir to combine.
5. Cook the black beans, stirring occasionally, for 5-7 minutes, or until heated through and well seasoned.
6. Mash some of the black beans with the back of a spoon or a potato masher to thicken the mixture slightly.

7. Remove the skillet from the heat and stir in the lime juice and chopped fresh cilantro.
8. Warm the tortillas according to package instructions.
9. To assemble the tacos, spoon some of the black bean mixture onto each tortilla.
10. Top the black beans with your desired toppings, such as shredded lettuce, diced tomatoes, diced avocado, sliced jalapeños, chopped cilantro, vegan sour cream, salsa, or lime wedges.
11. Serve the black bean tacos immediately, with extra toppings on the side.
12. Enjoy your homemade black bean tacos as a delicious and satisfying meal!

Feel free to customize the black bean tacos recipe by adding other ingredients such as corn kernels, diced bell peppers, shredded vegan cheese, or your favorite hot sauce. You can also use crunchy taco shells instead of soft tortillas for a different texture.

Stuffed bell peppers

Ingredients:

- 4 large bell peppers (any color), halved and seeds removed
- 1 tablespoon olive oil
- 1 onion, chopped
- 2 cloves garlic, minced
- 1 carrot, diced
- 1 zucchini, diced
- 1 cup cooked quinoa or rice
- 1 can (15 ounces) black beans, drained and rinsed
- 1 cup corn kernels (fresh, frozen, or canned)
- 1 cup diced tomatoes (fresh or canned)
- 1 teaspoon ground cumin
- 1 teaspoon chili powder
- 1/2 teaspoon smoked paprika
- Salt and black pepper, to taste
- 1 cup shredded vegan cheese or regular cheese (optional)
- Chopped fresh cilantro, for garnish (optional)
- Sliced green onions, for garnish (optional)
- Sliced avocado, for serving (optional)
- Vegan sour cream or regular sour cream, for serving (optional)

Instructions:

1. Preheat your oven to 375°F (190°C). Grease a baking dish with olive oil or cooking spray.
2. Heat the olive oil in a large skillet over medium heat.
3. Add the chopped onion to the skillet and sauté until softened and translucent, about 5 minutes.
4. Stir in the minced garlic and cook for an additional 1-2 minutes, until fragrant.
5. Add the diced carrot and diced zucchini to the skillet. Cook for 5-7 minutes, or until the vegetables are tender.
6. Stir in the cooked quinoa or rice, black beans, corn kernels, diced tomatoes, ground cumin, chili powder, smoked paprika, salt, and black pepper. Cook for an

additional 2-3 minutes, until everything is heated through and well combined. Taste and adjust seasoning, if needed.
7. Arrange the halved bell peppers in the prepared baking dish, cut side up.
8. Spoon the quinoa and vegetable mixture evenly into each bell pepper half, pressing down gently to pack the filling.
9. If using, sprinkle the shredded vegan cheese or regular cheese over the top of each stuffed bell pepper.
10. Cover the baking dish with aluminum foil and bake the stuffed bell peppers in the preheated oven for 25-30 minutes, or until the peppers are tender and the filling is heated through.
11. Remove the foil and bake for an additional 5-10 minutes, or until the cheese is melted and bubbly.
12. Once cooked, remove the stuffed bell peppers from the oven and let them cool for a few minutes.
13. Garnish the stuffed bell peppers with chopped fresh cilantro and sliced green onions, if desired.
14. Serve the stuffed bell peppers hot, with sliced avocado and vegan sour cream or regular sour cream on the side, if desired.
15. Enjoy your homemade stuffed bell peppers as a delicious and satisfying meal!

Feel free to customize the stuffed bell peppers recipe by adding other ingredients such as diced mushrooms, spinach, or cooked lentils for extra flavor and nutrition. You can also adjust the level of spiciness by adding more or less chili powder or smoked paprika according to your taste preferences.

Vegan shepherd's pie

Ingredients:

For the mashed potatoes:

- 2 pounds potatoes, peeled and chopped
- 1/4 cup vegan butter or olive oil
- 1/2 cup unsweetened non-dairy milk (such as almond milk or soy milk)
- Salt and black pepper, to taste

For the filling:

- 1 tablespoon olive oil
- 1 onion, chopped
- 2 cloves garlic, minced
- 2 carrots, diced
- 2 celery stalks, diced
- 8 ounces mushrooms, chopped
- 1 can (15 ounces) lentils, drained and rinsed
- 1 cup frozen peas
- 2 tablespoons tomato paste
- 1 tablespoon soy sauce or tamari
- 1 teaspoon dried thyme
- 1 teaspoon dried rosemary
- Salt and black pepper, to taste
- 1 cup vegetable broth
- 2 tablespoons cornstarch mixed with 2 tablespoons water (optional, for thickening)

Instructions:

1. Preheat your oven to 400°F (200°C).
2. Place the chopped potatoes in a large pot and cover them with water. Bring the water to a boil over high heat, then reduce the heat to medium-low and simmer for 10-15 minutes, or until the potatoes are fork-tender.

3. While the potatoes are cooking, heat the olive oil in a large skillet over medium heat.
4. Add the chopped onion to the skillet and sauté until softened and translucent, about 5 minutes.
5. Stir in the minced garlic and cook for an additional 1-2 minutes, until fragrant.
6. Add the diced carrots and diced celery to the skillet. Cook for 5-7 minutes, or until the vegetables are tender.
7. Add the chopped mushrooms to the skillet and cook for another 5 minutes, or until they are softened and golden brown.
8. Stir in the drained and rinsed lentils, frozen peas, tomato paste, soy sauce or tamari, dried thyme, dried rosemary, salt, and black pepper. Cook for 2-3 minutes, stirring frequently, to allow the flavors to meld together.
9. Pour in the vegetable broth and simmer the mixture for 5-7 minutes, until the liquid has reduced slightly. If desired, stir in the cornstarch mixture to thicken the filling.
10. Once cooked, remove the skillet from the heat.
11. Drain the cooked potatoes and return them to the pot. Add the vegan butter or olive oil and non-dairy milk to the pot. Mash the potatoes until smooth and creamy. Season with salt and black pepper, to taste.
12. Transfer the lentil and vegetable mixture to a large baking dish and spread it out evenly.
13. Spoon the mashed potatoes over the top of the lentil mixture, spreading them out into an even layer.
14. Use a fork to create ridges on the surface of the mashed potatoes.
15. Place the baking dish in the preheated oven and bake the vegan shepherd's pie for 25-30 minutes, or until the mashed potatoes are golden brown and the filling is bubbly.
16. Once cooked, remove the vegan shepherd's pie from the oven and let it cool for a few minutes before serving.
17. Serve the vegan shepherd's pie hot, with your favorite sides or a simple green salad.
18. Enjoy your homemade vegan shepherd's pie as a delicious and comforting meal!

Feel free to customize the vegan shepherd's pie recipe by adding other vegetables such as corn, green beans, or bell peppers to the filling. You can also experiment with different herbs and spices to suit your taste preferences.

Eggplant parmesan

Ingredients:

- 2 large eggplants, sliced into 1/2-inch rounds
- Salt
- 2 cups all-purpose flour
- 4 large eggs, beaten
- 2 cups breadcrumbs (plain or Italian seasoned)
- 1 cup grated Parmesan cheese (plus extra for serving)
- 2 cups marinara sauce (homemade or store-bought)
- 2 cups shredded mozzarella cheese
- Fresh basil leaves, chopped (for garnish, optional)
- Olive oil, for frying

Instructions:

1. Preheat your oven to 375°F (190°C).
2. Place the eggplant slices in a colander and sprinkle them generously with salt. Let them sit for about 30 minutes to draw out excess moisture. Rinse the eggplant slices under cold water and pat them dry with paper towels.
3. Set up a breading station with three shallow bowls: one with all-purpose flour, one with beaten eggs, and one with a mixture of breadcrumbs and grated Parmesan cheese.
4. Dip each eggplant slice into the flour, shaking off any excess, then dip it into the beaten eggs, and finally coat it in the breadcrumb-Parmesan mixture. Press gently to adhere the breadcrumbs to the eggplant.
5. Heat a thin layer of olive oil in a large skillet over medium heat. Working in batches, fry the breaded eggplant slices until golden brown and crispy on both sides, about 3-4 minutes per side. Transfer the fried eggplant slices to a paper towel-lined plate to drain any excess oil.
6. Spread a thin layer of marinara sauce on the bottom of a baking dish.
7. Arrange a single layer of fried eggplant slices on top of the marinara sauce.
8. Spoon more marinara sauce over the eggplant slices, then sprinkle a layer of shredded mozzarella cheese on top.
9. Repeat the layers of eggplant, marinara sauce, and mozzarella cheese until all the ingredients are used, ending with a layer of mozzarella cheese on top.

10. Cover the baking dish with aluminum foil and bake the eggplant Parmesan in the preheated oven for 25-30 minutes, or until the cheese is melted and bubbly.
11. Remove the foil and continue baking for an additional 5-10 minutes, or until the cheese is golden brown and bubbly.
12. Once cooked, remove the eggplant Parmesan from the oven and let it cool for a few minutes before serving.
13. Garnish with chopped fresh basil leaves and extra grated Parmesan cheese, if desired.
14. Serve the eggplant Parmesan hot, with your favorite pasta or a side salad.
15. Enjoy your homemade eggplant Parmesan as a delicious and comforting meal!

Feel free to customize the eggplant Parmesan recipe by adding other ingredients such as sliced tomatoes, roasted red peppers, or fresh herbs to the layers. You can also use a combination of different cheeses like provolone or fontina for added flavor.

Vegan pad thai

Ingredients:

For the Pad Thai sauce:

- 1/4 cup soy sauce or tamari
- 2 tablespoons maple syrup or brown sugar
- 2 tablespoons rice vinegar
- 1 tablespoon lime juice
- 1 tablespoon tamarind paste
- 1 teaspoon sriracha sauce (adjust to taste)
- 2 cloves garlic, minced
- 1 teaspoon grated ginger

For the Pad Thai:

- 8 ounces rice noodles
- 2 tablespoons vegetable oil
- 1 onion, thinly sliced
- 2 carrots, julienned
- 1 red bell pepper, thinly sliced
- 1 cup broccoli florets
- 1 cup tofu, cubed
- 2 green onions, sliced
- 1/4 cup chopped peanuts or cashews (optional)
- Fresh cilantro, for garnish (optional)
- Lime wedges, for serving

Instructions:

1. In a small bowl, whisk together all the ingredients for the Pad Thai sauce: soy sauce or tamari, maple syrup or brown sugar, rice vinegar, lime juice, tamarind paste, sriracha sauce, minced garlic, and grated ginger. Set aside.
2. Cook the rice noodles according to the package instructions until al dente. Drain and rinse under cold water to prevent sticking. Set aside.
3. Heat the vegetable oil in a large skillet or wok over medium-high heat.

4. Add the thinly sliced onion, julienned carrots, sliced red bell pepper, and broccoli florets to the skillet. Stir-fry for 3-4 minutes, or until the vegetables are tender-crisp.
5. Push the vegetables to one side of the skillet and add the cubed tofu to the empty space. Cook for 2-3 minutes, or until the tofu is golden brown on all sides.
6. Add the cooked rice noodles and sliced green onions to the skillet. Pour the Pad Thai sauce over the noodles and tofu. Toss everything together until well combined and heated through.
7. Taste the Pad Thai and adjust the seasoning if needed. If you prefer a sweeter Pad Thai, you can add more maple syrup or brown sugar.
8. Once heated through, remove the skillet from the heat.
9. Serve the vegan Pad Thai hot, garnished with chopped peanuts or cashews, fresh cilantro, and lime wedges on the side.
10. Enjoy your homemade vegan Pad Thai as a delicious and satisfying meal!

Feel free to customize the vegan Pad Thai recipe by adding other vegetables such as bean sprouts, snow peas, or mushrooms. You can also add protein options like tempeh or seitan instead of tofu. Adjust the spiciness level according to your preference by adding more or less sriracha sauce.

Ratatouille

Ingredients:

- 2 tablespoons olive oil
- 1 onion, diced
- 2 cloves garlic, minced
- 1 eggplant, diced
- 2 zucchini, diced
- 1 red bell pepper, diced
- 1 yellow bell pepper, diced
- 2 tomatoes, diced
- 1 can (14 ounces) diced tomatoes
- 1 tablespoon tomato paste
- 1 teaspoon dried thyme
- 1 teaspoon dried oregano
- Salt and black pepper, to taste
- Fresh basil leaves, chopped, for garnish (optional)

Instructions:

1. Heat the olive oil in a large skillet or Dutch oven over medium heat.
2. Add the diced onion to the skillet and sauté until softened and translucent, about 5 minutes.
3. Stir in the minced garlic and cook for an additional 1-2 minutes, until fragrant.
4. Add the diced eggplant to the skillet and cook for 5-7 minutes, or until it begins to soften.
5. Stir in the diced zucchini, diced red bell pepper, and diced yellow bell pepper. Cook for another 5 minutes, or until the vegetables are tender.
6. Add the diced tomatoes, canned diced tomatoes (with their juices), tomato paste, dried thyme, dried oregano, salt, and black pepper to the skillet. Stir to combine.
7. Bring the mixture to a simmer, then reduce the heat to low. Cover and let the ratatouille simmer gently for 20-30 minutes, stirring occasionally, until the flavors meld together and the vegetables are tender.
8. Taste the ratatouille and adjust the seasoning with salt and black pepper, if needed.
9. Once cooked, remove the skillet from the heat.

10. Serve the ratatouille hot, garnished with chopped fresh basil leaves, if desired.
11. Enjoy your homemade ratatouille as a delicious and wholesome meal!

Feel free to customize the ratatouille recipe by adding other vegetables such as mushrooms, carrots, or potatoes. You can also experiment with different herbs and spices to suit your taste preferences. Ratatouille can be served as a main dish with crusty bread or cooked grains, or as a side dish alongside grilled meats or fish.

Lentil shepherd's pie

Ingredients:

For the lentil filling:

- 1 cup dried green or brown lentils, rinsed and drained
- 3 cups vegetable broth
- 1 tablespoon olive oil
- 1 onion, diced
- 2 carrots, diced
- 2 celery stalks, diced
- 2 cloves garlic, minced
- 1 teaspoon dried thyme
- 1 teaspoon dried rosemary
- 1 teaspoon smoked paprika
- Salt and black pepper, to taste
- 1 cup frozen peas
- 1 cup corn kernels (fresh, frozen, or canned)
- 2 tablespoons tomato paste
- 2 tablespoons soy sauce or tamari
- 2 tablespoons all-purpose flour or cornstarch (for thickening, optional)

For the mashed potato topping:

- 2 pounds potatoes, peeled and chopped
- 1/4 cup vegan butter or olive oil
- 1/2 cup unsweetened non-dairy milk (such as almond milk or soy milk)
- Salt and black pepper, to taste

Instructions:

1. Preheat your oven to 375°F (190°C).
2. In a large saucepan, combine the rinsed lentils and vegetable broth. Bring the mixture to a boil over high heat, then reduce the heat to medium-low and simmer

for 20-25 minutes, or until the lentils are tender and most of the liquid is absorbed. Drain any excess liquid and set the cooked lentils aside.
3. While the lentils are cooking, prepare the mashed potato topping. Place the chopped potatoes in a large pot and cover them with water. Bring the water to a boil over high heat, then reduce the heat to medium-low and simmer for 15-20 minutes, or until the potatoes are fork-tender. Drain the cooked potatoes and return them to the pot.
4. Add the vegan butter or olive oil and non-dairy milk to the pot with the cooked potatoes. Mash the potatoes until smooth and creamy. Season with salt and black pepper, to taste. Set aside.
5. In a large skillet or Dutch oven, heat the olive oil over medium heat. Add the diced onion, carrots, and celery to the skillet. Sauté until the vegetables are softened, about 5-7 minutes.
6. Stir in the minced garlic, dried thyme, dried rosemary, smoked paprika, salt, and black pepper. Cook for an additional 1-2 minutes, until fragrant.
7. Add the cooked lentils, frozen peas, corn kernels, tomato paste, and soy sauce or tamari to the skillet. Stir to combine.
8. If desired, sprinkle the flour or cornstarch over the lentil mixture and stir to thicken the filling. Cook for another 2-3 minutes, until the mixture is heated through and slightly thickened.
9. Transfer the lentil filling to a large baking dish and spread it out evenly.
10. Spoon the mashed potato topping over the lentil filling, spreading it out into an even layer.
11. Use a fork to create ridges on the surface of the mashed potatoes.
12. Place the baking dish in the preheated oven and bake the lentil shepherd's pie for 25-30 minutes, or until the mashed potatoes are golden brown and the filling is bubbly.
13. Once cooked, remove the lentil shepherd's pie from the oven and let it cool for a few minutes before serving.
14. Serve the lentil shepherd's pie hot, with your favorite sides or a simple green salad.
15. Enjoy your homemade lentil shepherd's pie as a delicious and comforting meal!

Feel free to customize the lentil shepherd's pie recipe by adding other vegetables such as mushrooms, bell peppers, or spinach to the filling. You can also experiment with different herbs and spices to suit your taste preferences.

Vegan stuffed shells

Ingredients:

- 1 box (12 ounces) jumbo pasta shells
- 1 block (14-16 ounces) firm tofu, drained and pressed
- 1 cup spinach, chopped
- 1 cup vegan ricotta cheese
- 1/4 cup nutritional yeast
- 2 cloves garlic, minced
- 1 teaspoon dried basil
- 1 teaspoon dried oregano
- 1/2 teaspoon onion powder
- Salt and pepper to taste
- 1 jar (24 ounces) marinara sauce

Instructions:

1. Preheat your oven to 375°F (190°C). Cook the pasta shells according to the package instructions until al dente. Drain and set aside.
2. In a large mixing bowl, crumble the tofu using your hands or a fork. Add the chopped spinach, vegan ricotta cheese, nutritional yeast, minced garlic, dried basil, dried oregano, onion powder, salt, and pepper. Mix everything together until well combined.
3. Spread a thin layer of marinara sauce on the bottom of a baking dish.
4. Stuff each cooked shell with the tofu and spinach mixture, and place them in the baking dish.
5. Once all shells are stuffed and placed in the baking dish, pour the remaining marinara sauce over the top, covering all the shells.
6. Cover the baking dish with foil and bake in the preheated oven for 25-30 minutes, or until the shells are heated through and the sauce is bubbly.
7. Remove from the oven and let cool for a few minutes before serving.
8. Optionally, garnish with fresh basil or parsley before serving.

Enjoy your delicious vegan stuffed shells!

Veggie burgers

Ingredients:

- 1 can (15 ounces) black beans, drained and rinsed
- 1 cup cooked quinoa or brown rice
- 1/2 cup finely chopped onion
- 1/2 cup grated carrots
- 1/2 cup finely chopped bell pepper (any color)
- 2 cloves garlic, minced
- 1/4 cup chopped fresh parsley or cilantro
- 1 teaspoon ground cumin
- 1 teaspoon paprika
- 1/2 teaspoon chili powder (optional, for extra spice)
- Salt and pepper to taste
- 1/2 cup breadcrumbs (adjust as needed)
- Olive oil for cooking

Instructions:

1. In a large mixing bowl, mash the black beans with a fork or potato masher until mostly smooth, leaving some chunks for texture.
2. Add the cooked quinoa or brown rice, chopped onion, grated carrots, chopped bell pepper, minced garlic, chopped parsley or cilantro, ground cumin, paprika, chili powder (if using), salt, and pepper to the bowl. Mix everything together until well combined.
3. Gradually add the breadcrumbs to the mixture until it reaches a consistency that holds together well. You may need more or less breadcrumbs depending on the moisture content of the mixture.
4. Divide the mixture into equal portions and shape them into burger patties. You should get around 4-6 patties, depending on the size you prefer.
5. Heat a drizzle of olive oil in a skillet over medium heat. Once hot, add the veggie burger patties to the skillet (you may need to cook them in batches depending on the size of your skillet).
6. Cook the patties for 4-5 minutes on each side, or until golden brown and heated through.

7. Once cooked, remove the veggie burgers from the skillet and let them cool slightly before serving.
8. Serve the veggie burgers on buns with your favorite toppings such as lettuce, tomato, avocado, onion, and condiments like vegan mayo or mustard.

Enjoy your homemade veggie burgers!

Vegan spaghetti carbonara

Ingredients:

- 12 ounces (about 340g) spaghetti (use gluten-free if needed)
- 1 cup raw cashews, soaked in hot water for at least 1 hour or overnight
- 1 cup unsweetened almond milk (or any other plant-based milk)
- 2 tablespoons nutritional yeast
- 2 tablespoons lemon juice
- 2 cloves garlic, minced
- 1/2 teaspoon turmeric powder (for color)
- Salt and black pepper to taste
- 1 tablespoon olive oil
- 1 small onion, finely chopped
- 1 cup sliced mushrooms (optional)
- 1 cup frozen green peas, thawed
- Vegan bacon or tempeh bacon, chopped (optional)
- Fresh parsley, chopped, for garnish (optional)

Instructions:

1. Cook the spaghetti according to the package instructions until al dente. Drain and set aside, reserving about 1/2 cup of the pasta water.
2. In a blender, combine the soaked cashews (drained), almond milk, nutritional yeast, lemon juice, minced garlic, turmeric powder, salt, and black pepper. Blend until smooth and creamy. Set aside.
3. Heat olive oil in a large skillet over medium heat. Add the chopped onion and sauté until translucent, about 3-4 minutes.
4. If using, add the sliced mushrooms to the skillet and cook until they release their moisture and start to brown, about 5 minutes.
5. Add the cooked spaghetti to the skillet along with the thawed green peas and vegan bacon or tempeh bacon (if using). Stir to combine.
6. Pour the cashew cream sauce over the spaghetti mixture in the skillet. Stir well to coat the spaghetti evenly with the sauce. If the sauce is too thick, gradually add some of the reserved pasta water until you reach your desired consistency.
7. Cook the spaghetti carbonara for another 2-3 minutes, stirring frequently, until heated through.

8. Remove from heat and serve the vegan spaghetti carbonara hot, garnished with chopped fresh parsley if desired.

Enjoy your creamy and delicious vegan spaghetti carbonara!

Cauliflower buffalo wings

Ingredients:

For the cauliflower:

- 1 medium head cauliflower, cut into florets
- 1 cup all-purpose flour (or chickpea flour for a gluten-free option)
- 1 cup water
- 1 teaspoon garlic powder
- 1 teaspoon onion powder
- 1/2 teaspoon paprika
- Salt and pepper to taste

For the buffalo sauce:

- 1/2 cup hot sauce (such as Frank's RedHot)
- 1/4 cup vegan butter or margarine
- 1 tablespoon apple cider vinegar
- 1 teaspoon garlic powder
- 1 teaspoon paprika

Instructions:

1. Preheat your oven to 450°F (230°C). Line a baking sheet with parchment paper or lightly grease it with oil.
2. In a large mixing bowl, whisk together the flour, water, garlic powder, onion powder, paprika, salt, and pepper until you have a smooth batter.
3. Dip each cauliflower floret into the batter, making sure it's evenly coated, then place it on the prepared baking sheet. Repeat until all florets are coated and arranged in a single layer on the baking sheet.
4. Bake the cauliflower in the preheated oven for 20-25 minutes, or until golden brown and crispy, flipping halfway through the cooking time.
5. While the cauliflower is baking, prepare the buffalo sauce. In a small saucepan, melt the vegan butter over low heat. Once melted, stir in the hot sauce, apple

cider vinegar, garlic powder, and paprika. Cook for a few minutes, stirring occasionally, until the sauce is heated through and well combined.
6. Once the cauliflower is done baking, remove it from the oven and transfer the florets to a large mixing bowl. Pour the buffalo sauce over the cauliflower and toss until each floret is evenly coated with the sauce.
7. Return the cauliflower to the baking sheet and bake for an additional 10-15 minutes, or until the sauce is caramelized and the cauliflower is crispy around the edges.
8. Remove from the oven and let cool slightly before serving. Serve your cauliflower buffalo wings with vegan ranch or blue cheese dressing and celery sticks for a classic appetizer experience.

Enjoy your delicious and spicy cauliflower buffalo wings!

Vegan sushi rolls

Ingredients:

- Sushi rice
- Nori sheets (seaweed)
- Fillings of your choice (options include avocado, cucumber, carrot, bell pepper, tofu, asparagus, mango, and more)
- Soy sauce or tamari for dipping
- Wasabi (optional)
- Pickled ginger (optional)

Instructions:

1. Prepare sushi rice according to package instructions. Make sure to rinse the rice thoroughly before cooking to remove excess starch. Once cooked, season the rice with a mixture of rice vinegar, sugar, and salt to taste. Allow the rice to cool to room temperature.
2. While the rice is cooling, prepare your fillings. Slice your chosen vegetables or fruits into thin strips or julienne them for easy rolling.
3. Lay a sheet of nori on a bamboo sushi rolling mat or a clean kitchen towel with the shiny side facing down.
4. Spread a thin layer of sushi rice evenly over the nori sheet, leaving about 1 inch of the nori sheet uncovered at the top.
5. Arrange your fillings in a line across the center of the rice-covered nori sheet.
6. Using the bamboo mat or towel, carefully roll the nori sheet over the fillings, applying gentle pressure to shape the roll. Roll tightly to ensure the ingredients stay together.
7. Moisten the exposed edge of the nori sheet with a bit of water to seal the roll.
8. Using a sharp knife, slice the roll into individual pieces, wiping the knife clean between cuts to ensure neat slices.
9. Serve the vegan sushi rolls with soy sauce or tamari for dipping, along with wasabi and pickled ginger if desired.

Feel free to get creative with your fillings and experiment with different combinations to suit your taste preferences. Enjoy your homemade vegan sushi rolls!

Butternut squash soup

Ingredients:

- 1 medium-sized butternut squash, peeled, seeded, and diced
- 1 onion, chopped
- 2 cloves garlic, minced
- 1 medium carrot, chopped
- 1 medium potato, peeled and diced
- 4 cups vegetable broth
- 1 teaspoon ground cumin
- 1/2 teaspoon ground cinnamon
- 1/4 teaspoon ground nutmeg
- Salt and pepper to taste
- Olive oil
- Optional garnishes: chopped fresh parsley, coconut cream, pumpkin seeds

Instructions:

1. Heat a tablespoon of olive oil in a large pot over medium heat. Add the chopped onion and cook until softened, about 5 minutes.
2. Add the minced garlic and cook for another minute until fragrant.
3. Add the diced butternut squash, carrot, and potato to the pot. Stir to combine with the onion and garlic.
4. Pour in the vegetable broth, ensuring that the vegetables are mostly covered. Bring the mixture to a boil, then reduce the heat to low and let it simmer for about 20-25 minutes, or until the vegetables are tender.
5. Once the vegetables are cooked through, use an immersion blender to blend the soup until smooth. Alternatively, you can transfer the soup in batches to a blender and blend until smooth, then return it to the pot.
6. Stir in the ground cumin, cinnamon, and nutmeg. Season with salt and pepper to taste, adjusting the seasoning as needed.
7. Continue to cook the soup over low heat for another 5-10 minutes to allow the flavors to meld together.
8. Serve the butternut squash soup hot, garnished with chopped fresh parsley, a drizzle of coconut cream, and/or pumpkin seeds if desired.

This butternut squash soup is delicious on its own or paired with a slice of crusty bread for a comforting meal. Enjoy!

Sweet potato casserole

Ingredients:

For the sweet potato base:

- 4-5 medium sweet potatoes, peeled and cubed
- 1/2 cup granulated sugar
- 2 large eggs, lightly beaten
- 1/2 cup milk (you can use dairy or non-dairy milk)
- 1/4 cup melted butter or vegan butter
- 1 teaspoon vanilla extract
- 1/2 teaspoon salt

For the topping:

- 1 cup packed brown sugar
- 1/3 cup all-purpose flour
- 1/3 cup melted butter or vegan butter
- 1 cup chopped pecans or walnuts (optional)

Instructions:

1. Preheat your oven to 350°F (175°C) and grease a baking dish (9x13 inch) with butter or cooking spray.
2. Place the peeled and cubed sweet potatoes in a large pot of water. Bring to a boil, then reduce the heat to medium-low and simmer for about 15-20 minutes, or until the sweet potatoes are tender when pierced with a fork.
3. Drain the sweet potatoes and transfer them to a large mixing bowl. Mash them until smooth using a potato masher or fork.
4. To the mashed sweet potatoes, add the granulated sugar, beaten eggs, milk, melted butter, vanilla extract, and salt. Stir until well combined.
5. Transfer the sweet potato mixture to the prepared baking dish, spreading it out evenly.
6. In a separate bowl, combine the brown sugar, flour, melted butter, and chopped pecans (if using) to make the topping. Mix until the mixture resembles coarse crumbs.
7. Sprinkle the topping evenly over the sweet potato mixture in the baking dish.
8. Bake in the preheated oven for 30-35 minutes, or until the topping is golden brown and the casserole is heated through.
9. Remove from the oven and let it cool for a few minutes before serving.

Enjoy this sweet and indulgent sweet potato casserole as a side dish for your holiday meals or any special occasion!

Vegan mushroom stroganoff

Ingredients:

- 12 oz (340g) pasta of your choice (such as fettuccine, tagliatelle, or penne)
- 2 tablespoons olive oil
- 1 onion, finely chopped
- 3 cloves garlic, minced
- 16 oz (450g) mushrooms, sliced (button mushrooms, cremini, or a mix)
- 1 tablespoon soy sauce or tamari
- 1 teaspoon dried thyme
- 1 teaspoon smoked paprika
- Salt and pepper to taste
- 1 cup vegetable broth
- 1 cup unsweetened non-dairy milk (such as almond milk or cashew milk)
- 2 tablespoons all-purpose flour or cornstarch (for thickening)
- 1 tablespoon Dijon mustard
- 2 tablespoons nutritional yeast (optional, for added flavor)
- Fresh parsley, chopped, for garnish (optional)

Instructions:

1. Cook the pasta according to the package instructions until al dente. Drain and set aside.
2. Heat the olive oil in a large skillet over medium heat. Add the chopped onion and cook until softened, about 3-4 minutes.
3. Add the minced garlic to the skillet and cook for another minute until fragrant.
4. Add the sliced mushrooms to the skillet and cook, stirring occasionally, until they release their moisture and start to brown, about 8-10 minutes.
5. Stir in the soy sauce or tamari, dried thyme, smoked paprika, salt, and pepper. Cook for another minute to let the flavors meld together.
6. In a small bowl, whisk together the vegetable broth, non-dairy milk, and flour or cornstarch until smooth. Pour this mixture into the skillet, stirring constantly.
7. Bring the mixture to a simmer and cook for 5-7 minutes, or until the sauce thickens.
8. Stir in the Dijon mustard and nutritional yeast (if using) until well combined. Taste and adjust seasoning if needed.

9. Add the cooked pasta to the skillet and toss until evenly coated with the mushroom sauce.
10. Serve the vegan mushroom stroganoff hot, garnished with chopped fresh parsley if desired.

This vegan mushroom stroganoff is creamy, flavorful, and sure to please vegans and non-vegans alike!

Lentil meatballs

Ingredients:

For the lentil meatballs:

- 1 cup dried brown lentils
- 2 cups vegetable broth or water
- 1 small onion, finely chopped
- 3 cloves garlic, minced
- 1 carrot, grated
- 1/4 cup chopped fresh parsley
- 1 tablespoon tomato paste
- 1 tablespoon soy sauce or tamari
- 1 teaspoon dried oregano
- 1 teaspoon dried basil
- 1/2 teaspoon smoked paprika
- 1/2 teaspoon salt
- 1/4 teaspoon black pepper
- 1/2 cup breadcrumbs (gluten-free if needed)
- 2 tablespoons olive oil, for cooking

For the tomato sauce (optional):

- 1 can (14 oz) crushed tomatoes
- 2 cloves garlic, minced
- 1 teaspoon dried oregano
- Salt and pepper to taste

Instructions:

1. Rinse the lentils under cold water. In a medium saucepan, combine the lentils and vegetable broth or water. Bring to a boil, then reduce the heat to low and simmer, covered, for about 20-25 minutes, or until the lentils are tender and most of the liquid is absorbed. Drain any excess liquid and let the lentils cool slightly.

2. Preheat your oven to 375°F (190°C) and line a baking sheet with parchment paper.
3. In a large mixing bowl, mash the cooked lentils using a potato masher or fork. You want them to be somewhat mashed but still have texture.
4. Add the chopped onion, minced garlic, grated carrot, chopped parsley, tomato paste, soy sauce or tamari, dried oregano, dried basil, smoked paprika, salt, black pepper, and breadcrumbs to the bowl with the mashed lentils. Mix until well combined.
5. Form the lentil mixture into golf ball-sized meatballs and place them on the prepared baking sheet.
6. Drizzle the lentil meatballs with olive oil and bake in the preheated oven for 25-30 minutes, or until golden brown and firm to the touch.
7. While the lentil meatballs are baking, you can prepare the tomato sauce if desired. In a saucepan, combine the crushed tomatoes, minced garlic, dried oregano, salt, and pepper. Bring to a simmer and cook for 5-10 minutes, stirring occasionally.
8. Serve the lentil meatballs hot, either on their own or with the tomato sauce spooned over the top. Enjoy!

These lentil meatballs are packed with flavor and protein, making them a nutritious and satisfying option for vegans and meat-eaters alike.

Vegan BBQ pulled jackfruit

Ingredients:

- 2 cans (20 oz each) young green jackfruit in water or brine, drained and rinsed
- 1 tablespoon olive oil
- 1 onion, diced
- 3 cloves garlic, minced
- 1 cup barbecue sauce (store-bought or homemade)
- 1/2 cup vegetable broth
- 2 tablespoons tomato paste
- 1 tablespoon soy sauce or tamari
- 1 tablespoon maple syrup or brown sugar
- 1 teaspoon smoked paprika
- 1/2 teaspoon chili powder
- Salt and pepper to taste
- Hamburger buns or sandwich rolls, for serving
- Coleslaw, pickles, or other toppings of your choice

Instructions:

1. Heat the olive oil in a large skillet or pot over medium heat. Add the diced onion and cook until softened, about 5 minutes.
2. Add the minced garlic to the skillet and cook for another minute until fragrant.
3. Add the drained and rinsed jackfruit to the skillet. Using a potato masher or fork, break up the jackfruit into smaller pieces that resemble shredded meat.
4. In a small bowl, whisk together the barbecue sauce, vegetable broth, tomato paste, soy sauce or tamari, maple syrup or brown sugar, smoked paprika, chili powder, salt, and pepper.
5. Pour the barbecue sauce mixture over the shredded jackfruit in the skillet and stir to combine.
6. Bring the mixture to a simmer, then reduce the heat to low and let it cook uncovered for about 20-25 minutes, stirring occasionally, until the jackfruit is tender and the sauce has thickened.
7. Taste and adjust the seasoning if needed, adding more salt, pepper, or other spices to taste.

8. Once the jackfruit is cooked and the sauce has thickened to your liking, remove the skillet from the heat.
9. Serve the vegan BBQ pulled jackfruit on hamburger buns or sandwich rolls, topped with coleslaw, pickles, or your favorite toppings.
10. Enjoy your delicious vegan BBQ pulled jackfruit sandwiches!

This dish is perfect for BBQ lovers and vegetarians/vegans alike. It's flavorful, satisfying, and easy to make!

Vegan jambalaya

Ingredients:

- 1 tablespoon olive oil
- 1 onion, diced
- 3 cloves garlic, minced
- 1 bell pepper, diced (any color)
- 2 celery stalks, diced
- 1 cup diced tomatoes (fresh or canned)
- 1 cup long-grain white rice
- 2 cups vegetable broth
- 1 can (15 oz) kidney beans, drained and rinsed
- 1 can (15 oz) black-eyed peas, drained and rinsed
- 1 cup chopped okra (fresh or frozen)
- 1 tablespoon Cajun seasoning (adjust to taste)
- 1 teaspoon smoked paprika
- 1/2 teaspoon dried thyme
- Salt and pepper to taste
- Fresh parsley, chopped, for garnish (optional)
- Hot sauce, for serving (optional)

Instructions:

1. Heat the olive oil in a large skillet or pot over medium heat. Add the diced onion, minced garlic, diced bell pepper, and diced celery. Cook, stirring occasionally, until the vegetables are softened, about 5-7 minutes.
2. Add the diced tomatoes to the skillet and cook for another 2-3 minutes.
3. Stir in the long-grain white rice and cook for 1-2 minutes, stirring constantly to coat the rice with the vegetable mixture.
4. Pour in the vegetable broth and bring the mixture to a boil.
5. Once boiling, reduce the heat to low, cover, and let the jambalaya simmer for about 15-20 minutes, or until the rice is almost cooked through and most of the liquid is absorbed.
6. Stir in the drained and rinsed kidney beans, black-eyed peas, chopped okra, Cajun seasoning, smoked paprika, dried thyme, salt, and pepper.

7. Cover the skillet or pot again and continue to simmer for another 10-15 minutes, or until the rice is fully cooked and the flavors have melded together. If the mixture looks too dry, you can add a splash of vegetable broth or water.
8. Taste and adjust the seasoning if needed, adding more Cajun seasoning, salt, or pepper to taste.
9. Once the jambalaya is cooked to your liking, remove it from the heat and let it sit, covered, for a few minutes before serving.
10. Serve the vegan jambalaya hot, garnished with chopped fresh parsley if desired, and with hot sauce on the side for those who like it spicy.

Enjoy this delicious vegan jambalaya as a satisfying and flavorful meal that's packed with Cajun-inspired goodness!

Vegan gnocchi

Ingredients:

- 2 large russet potatoes (about 1.5 lbs or 700g)
- 1 to 1.5 cups all-purpose flour (plus extra for dusting)
- Salt, to taste

Instructions:

1. Start by washing the potatoes thoroughly and poking them several times with a fork. This allows steam to escape during cooking.
2. Place the potatoes in a large pot and cover them with water. Bring the water to a boil, then reduce the heat to a simmer and cook the potatoes until they are fork-tender, typically around 45 minutes to 1 hour.
3. Once the potatoes are cooked, drain them and let them cool slightly until you can handle them comfortably.
4. Peel the potatoes while they're still warm. Use a potato ricer or a fork to mash them until they're smooth and free of lumps. Allow the mashed potatoes to cool completely.
5. Once cooled, transfer the mashed potatoes to a clean, flat work surface. Gradually add the flour, starting with 1 cup, and knead it into the mashed potatoes until you have a soft, slightly sticky dough. Add more flour as needed, but be careful not to add too much, as this can make the gnocchi dense.
6. Divide the dough into smaller portions and roll each portion into a long, thin rope, about 1/2 inch (1 cm) in diameter.
7. Use a sharp knife to cut the ropes of dough into bite-sized pieces. You can leave them as is, or you can use a fork to make indentations on each piece to create traditional gnocchi ridges.
8. Bring a large pot of salted water to a boil. Once boiling, add the gnocchi in batches, being careful not to overcrowd the pot. Cook the gnocchi until they float to the surface, usually about 2-3 minutes.
9. Use a slotted spoon to remove the cooked gnocchi from the water and transfer them to a plate lined with a clean kitchen towel to drain.
10. Repeat the process with the remaining gnocchi until they're all cooked.

11. Serve the vegan gnocchi with your favorite sauce, such as marinara sauce, pesto, or a creamy vegan sauce. Garnish with fresh herbs and a sprinkle of vegan Parmesan cheese, if desired.

Enjoy your homemade vegan gnocchi!

Vegan meatloaf

Ingredients:

For the "meatloaf":

- 1 cup cooked brown lentils
- 1 cup cooked quinoa
- 1 onion, finely chopped
- 2 cloves garlic, minced
- 1 carrot, grated
- 1 celery stalk, finely chopped
- 1 bell pepper, finely chopped
- 1 cup breadcrumbs (gluten-free if needed)
- 1/4 cup tomato paste
- 2 tablespoons soy sauce or tamari
- 2 tablespoons ground flaxseeds mixed with 6 tablespoons water (flax eggs)
- 1 tablespoon Worcestershire sauce (make sure it's vegan)
- 1 teaspoon dried thyme
- 1 teaspoon dried oregano
- 1/2 teaspoon smoked paprika
- Salt and pepper to taste

For the glaze:

- 1/4 cup ketchup
- 2 tablespoons maple syrup
- 1 tablespoon apple cider vinegar
- 1 teaspoon Dijon mustard

Instructions:

1. Preheat your oven to 375°F (190°C). Grease a loaf pan with olive oil or line it with parchment paper.
2. In a large mixing bowl, combine the cooked brown lentils, cooked quinoa, chopped onion, minced garlic, grated carrot, chopped celery, chopped bell pepper,

breadcrumbs, tomato paste, soy sauce or tamari, flax eggs, Worcestershire sauce, dried thyme, dried oregano, smoked paprika, salt, and pepper. Mix until well combined.
3. Transfer the mixture to the prepared loaf pan, pressing it down firmly to pack it in.
4. In a small bowl, whisk together the ketchup, maple syrup, apple cider vinegar, and Dijon mustard to make the glaze.
5. Spread the glaze evenly over the top of the vegan meatloaf.
6. Bake the meatloaf in the preheated oven for 45-50 minutes, or until the top is golden brown and the edges are slightly crispy.
7. Remove the meatloaf from the oven and let it cool in the pan for about 10 minutes before slicing and serving.
8. Serve the vegan meatloaf slices with your favorite sides, such as mashed potatoes, steamed vegetables, or a green salad.

Enjoy your hearty and flavorful vegan meatloaf!

Chickpea salad sandwiches

Ingredients:

- 1 can (15 oz) chickpeas (garbanzo beans), drained and rinsed
- 2 tablespoons vegan mayonnaise
- 1 tablespoon Dijon mustard
- 1 tablespoon lemon juice
- 2 stalks celery, finely chopped
- 1/4 cup red onion, finely chopped
- 2 tablespoons fresh parsley, chopped
- Salt and pepper to taste
- Bread or sandwich rolls of your choice
- Lettuce leaves, tomato slices, avocado slices, or any other sandwich toppings you like

Instructions:

1. In a large mixing bowl, mash the chickpeas with a fork or potato masher until they're mostly mashed but still have some texture.
2. Add the vegan mayonnaise, Dijon mustard, and lemon juice to the mashed chickpeas. Stir until well combined.
3. Add the chopped celery, red onion, and fresh parsley to the bowl with the chickpea mixture. Mix until everything is evenly distributed.
4. Taste the chickpea salad and season with salt and pepper to taste. Adjust the seasoning as needed.
5. Toast your bread or sandwich rolls if desired.
6. Assemble your sandwiches by spreading a generous amount of the chickpea salad onto one slice of bread or the bottom half of a sandwich roll.
7. Top the chickpea salad with lettuce leaves, tomato slices, avocado slices, or any other sandwich toppings you like.
8. Place the remaining slice of bread or the top half of the sandwich roll on top of the fillings to complete the sandwiches.
9. Slice the sandwiches in half if desired and serve immediately, or wrap them up and pack them for a delicious and portable lunch.

Enjoy your flavorful and satisfying chickpea salad sandwiches! They're perfect for lunch or a light dinner.

Vegan pesto pasta

Ingredients:

For the vegan pesto:

- 2 cups fresh basil leaves, packed
- 1/3 cup pine nuts or walnuts
- 3 cloves garlic, minced
- 1/4 cup nutritional yeast
- 1/4 cup extra-virgin olive oil
- 1 tablespoon lemon juice
- Salt and pepper to taste

For the pasta:

- 12 oz (340g) pasta of your choice (such as spaghetti, linguine, or penne)
- Salt for boiling water
- Cherry tomatoes, halved (optional)
- Fresh basil leaves, for garnish (optional)
- Vegan Parmesan cheese, for serving (optional)

Instructions:

1. Start by cooking the pasta according to the package instructions in a large pot of salted boiling water. Cook until al dente, then drain and set aside. Reserve about 1/2 cup of pasta cooking water.
2. While the pasta is cooking, prepare the vegan pesto. In a food processor or blender, combine the fresh basil leaves, pine nuts or walnuts, minced garlic, nutritional yeast, extra-virgin olive oil, lemon juice, salt, and pepper. Blend until smooth, scraping down the sides as needed. If the pesto is too thick, you can add a little water or more olive oil to reach your desired consistency.
3. Once the pasta is cooked and drained, return it to the pot. Add the vegan pesto to the pot with the cooked pasta, along with the reserved pasta cooking water. Toss until the pasta is evenly coated with the pesto sauce.
4. If desired, add halved cherry tomatoes to the pasta and toss to combine.

5. Serve the vegan pesto pasta hot, garnished with fresh basil leaves and vegan Parmesan cheese if desired.

Enjoy your delicious and flavorful vegan pesto pasta! It's perfect for a quick and satisfying meal any day of the week.

Jackfruit tacos

Ingredients:

For the jackfruit filling:

- 2 cans (20 oz each) young green jackfruit in water or brine, drained and rinsed
- 1 tablespoon olive oil
- 1 onion, diced
- 3 cloves garlic, minced
- 1 bell pepper, diced
- 1 tablespoon chili powder
- 1 teaspoon ground cumin
- 1/2 teaspoon smoked paprika
- 1/2 teaspoon dried oregano
- Salt and pepper to taste
- 1/4 cup vegetable broth or water
- Juice of 1 lime

For serving:

- Tortillas (corn or flour)
- Your favorite taco toppings, such as shredded lettuce, diced tomatoes, sliced avocado, chopped cilantro, salsa, hot sauce, vegan sour cream, lime wedges, etc.

Instructions:

1. Heat the olive oil in a large skillet over medium heat. Add the diced onion and cook until softened, about 5 minutes.
2. Add the minced garlic and diced bell pepper to the skillet, and cook for another 2-3 minutes until fragrant.
3. Drain and rinse the canned jackfruit, then use your hands or a fork to shred it into smaller pieces, resembling pulled meat.
4. Add the shredded jackfruit to the skillet with the onions, garlic, and bell pepper. Cook for 2-3 minutes, stirring occasionally.

5. Sprinkle the chili powder, ground cumin, smoked paprika, dried oregano, salt, and pepper over the jackfruit mixture. Stir to evenly coat the jackfruit with the spices.
6. Pour in the vegetable broth or water and lime juice, stirring to combine. Allow the jackfruit mixture to simmer for 10-15 minutes, or until the flavors meld together and the liquid has mostly evaporated.
7. Taste and adjust the seasoning if needed, adding more salt, pepper, or spices to taste.
8. Warm the tortillas in a dry skillet or microwave.
9. To assemble the tacos, spoon some of the jackfruit filling onto each tortilla. Top with your favorite taco toppings, such as shredded lettuce, diced tomatoes, sliced avocado, chopped cilantro, salsa, hot sauce, vegan sour cream, and a squeeze of lime juice.
10. Serve the jackfruit tacos immediately and enjoy!

These jackfruit tacos are flavorful, satisfying, and perfect for a quick and easy weeknight meal or for entertaining guests.

Vegan moussaka

Ingredients:

For the eggplant layer:

- 2 large eggplants, sliced into rounds
- Salt
- Olive oil, for brushing

For the lentil filling:

- 1 cup dry green or brown lentils
- 2 cups vegetable broth or water
- 1 onion, finely chopped
- 3 cloves garlic, minced
- 1 carrot, grated
- 1 celery stalk, finely chopped
- 1 can (14 oz) diced tomatoes
- 2 tablespoons tomato paste
- 1 teaspoon dried oregano
- 1 teaspoon dried thyme
- Salt and pepper to taste

For the béchamel sauce:

- 1/4 cup vegan butter or olive oil
- 1/4 cup all-purpose flour (or gluten-free flour blend)
- 2 cups unsweetened non-dairy milk (such as almond milk or soy milk)
- 1/4 cup nutritional yeast
- 1/2 teaspoon ground nutmeg
- Salt and pepper to taste

Instructions:

1. Preheat your oven to 400°F (200°C). Line a baking sheet with parchment paper.
2. Place the sliced eggplant rounds on the prepared baking sheet. Sprinkle them with salt and let them sit for about 15 minutes to draw out excess moisture. Pat the eggplant slices dry with paper towels.
3. Brush both sides of the eggplant slices with olive oil. Bake in the preheated oven for 20-25 minutes, or until the eggplant is tender and slightly golden brown. Remove from the oven and set aside.
4. While the eggplant is baking, prepare the lentil filling. Rinse the lentils under cold water. In a medium saucepan, combine the lentils and vegetable broth or water. Bring to a boil, then reduce the heat to low and simmer for about 20-25 minutes, or until the lentils are tender and most of the liquid is absorbed.
5. In a large skillet, heat a little olive oil over medium heat. Add the chopped onion and cook until softened, about 5 minutes. Add the minced garlic and cook for another minute until fragrant.
6. Add the grated carrot and chopped celery to the skillet, and cook for another 5 minutes until softened.
7. Stir in the diced tomatoes, tomato paste, dried oregano, dried thyme, cooked lentils, salt, and pepper. Cook for another 5-10 minutes, stirring occasionally, until the mixture thickens slightly. Remove from heat and set aside.
8. To make the béchamel sauce, melt the vegan butter in a saucepan over medium heat. Whisk in the flour to form a paste (roux), and cook for 1-2 minutes, stirring constantly.
9. Gradually whisk in the non-dairy milk, nutritional yeast, and ground nutmeg. Continue to cook, stirring constantly, until the sauce thickens and becomes smooth, about 5-7 minutes. Season with salt and pepper to taste.
10. To assemble the moussaka, spread half of the lentil filling in the bottom of a 9x13 inch baking dish. Arrange half of the baked eggplant slices on top of the lentil filling.
11. Spread the remaining lentil filling over the eggplant slices, then top with the remaining eggplant slices.
12. Pour the béchamel sauce evenly over the top of the assembled moussaka.
13. Bake in the preheated oven for 30-35 minutes, or until the top is golden brown and bubbly.
14. Remove from the oven and let the moussaka cool for a few minutes before serving.
15. Serve the vegan moussaka warm, garnished with chopped fresh parsley if desired.

Enjoy this vegan moussaka as a hearty and flavorful main dish!

Vegan paella

Ingredients:

- 2 tablespoons olive oil
- 1 onion, diced
- 3 cloves garlic, minced
- 1 red bell pepper, diced
- 1 yellow bell pepper, diced
- 1 green bell pepper, diced
- 1 cup cherry tomatoes, halved
- 1 cup diced zucchini
- 1 cup diced eggplant
- 1 cup sliced mushrooms
- 1 1/2 cups Arborio rice (or other short-grain rice)
- 4 cups vegetable broth
- 1 teaspoon smoked paprika
- 1/2 teaspoon saffron threads (optional)
- Salt and pepper to taste
- 1 cup frozen peas
- 1/4 cup chopped fresh parsley
- Lemon wedges, for serving

Instructions:

1. Heat the olive oil in a large paella pan or skillet over medium heat. Add the diced onion and cook until softened, about 5 minutes.
2. Add the minced garlic to the pan and cook for another minute until fragrant.
3. Add the diced bell peppers, cherry tomatoes, diced zucchini, diced eggplant, and sliced mushrooms to the pan. Cook, stirring occasionally, for about 5-7 minutes, or until the vegetables start to soften.
4. Stir in the Arborio rice, smoked paprika, and saffron threads (if using), coating the rice evenly with the oil and spices.
5. Pour the vegetable broth into the pan and season with salt and pepper to taste. Stir gently to combine.

6. Bring the mixture to a simmer, then reduce the heat to low and let it cook, uncovered, for about 20-25 minutes, or until the rice is tender and most of the liquid is absorbed. Stir occasionally to prevent sticking and ensure even cooking.
7. Stir in the frozen peas during the last 5 minutes of cooking, allowing them to heat through.
8. Once the rice is cooked and the liquid is absorbed, remove the paella from the heat. Sprinkle chopped fresh parsley over the top.
9. Serve the vegan paella warm, garnished with lemon wedges for squeezing over the top.

Enjoy this flavorful and vibrant vegan paella as a delicious main dish that's sure to impress!

Vegan sloppy joes

Ingredients:

For the filling:

- 1 tablespoon olive oil
- 1 onion, diced
- 2 cloves garlic, minced
- 1 bell pepper, diced
- 1 carrot, grated
- 1 can (15 oz) lentils, drained and rinsed (or cooked lentils)
- 1 can (14 oz) diced tomatoes
- 2 tablespoons tomato paste
- 2 tablespoons maple syrup or brown sugar
- 2 tablespoons vegan Worcestershire sauce
- 1 tablespoon apple cider vinegar
- 1 teaspoon smoked paprika
- 1/2 teaspoon ground cumin
- Salt and pepper to taste

For serving:

- Hamburger buns or sandwich rolls
- Coleslaw or shredded cabbage (optional)
- Pickles (optional)

Instructions:

1. Heat the olive oil in a large skillet over medium heat. Add the diced onion and cook until softened, about 5 minutes.
2. Add the minced garlic and diced bell pepper to the skillet, and cook for another 2-3 minutes until fragrant.
3. Stir in the grated carrot and cook for another 2-3 minutes until softened.

4. Add the drained and rinsed lentils to the skillet, along with the diced tomatoes, tomato paste, maple syrup or brown sugar, vegan Worcestershire sauce, apple cider vinegar, smoked paprika, ground cumin, salt, and pepper. Stir to combine.
5. Bring the mixture to a simmer, then reduce the heat to low and let it cook for about 15-20 minutes, stirring occasionally, until the flavors meld together and the mixture thickens.
6. Taste and adjust the seasoning if needed, adding more salt, pepper, or spices to taste.
7. Once the filling is cooked and thickened to your liking, remove it from the heat.
8. To serve, spoon the vegan sloppy joe filling onto hamburger buns or sandwich rolls. Top with coleslaw or shredded cabbage for added crunch, and pickles if desired.
9. Serve the vegan sloppy joes hot and enjoy!

These vegan sloppy joes are flavorful, hearty, and perfect for a quick and satisfying meal.

Vegan pot pie

Ingredients:

For the filling:

- 2 tablespoons olive oil
- 1 onion, diced
- 2 cloves garlic, minced
- 2 carrots, diced
- 2 celery stalks, diced
- 1 cup diced potatoes
- 1 cup diced mushrooms
- 1 cup frozen peas
- 1/4 cup all-purpose flour (or gluten-free flour blend)
- 2 cups vegetable broth
- 1 cup unsweetened non-dairy milk (such as almond milk or soy milk)
- 1 tablespoon soy sauce or tamari
- 1 teaspoon dried thyme
- 1 teaspoon dried rosemary
- Salt and pepper to taste

For the crust:

- 1 1/2 cups all-purpose flour (or gluten-free flour blend)
- 1/2 cup vegan butter or vegetable shortening, chilled and cubed
- 1/4 cup ice water

Instructions:

1. Preheat your oven to 400°F (200°C).
2. To make the filling, heat the olive oil in a large skillet over medium heat. Add the diced onion and cook until softened, about 5 minutes.
3. Add the minced garlic to the skillet and cook for another minute until fragrant.
4. Add the diced carrots, diced celery, diced potatoes, and diced mushrooms to the skillet. Cook, stirring occasionally, for about 5-7 minutes until the vegetables start to soften.
5. Sprinkle the flour over the vegetables in the skillet and stir to coat evenly.

6. Gradually pour in the vegetable broth and non-dairy milk, stirring constantly to prevent lumps from forming. Bring the mixture to a simmer.
7. Stir in the frozen peas, soy sauce or tamari, dried thyme, dried rosemary, salt, and pepper. Cook for another 5-7 minutes until the filling thickens slightly. Remove from heat and set aside.
8. To make the crust, in a large mixing bowl, combine the flour and chilled vegan butter or vegetable shortening. Use a pastry cutter or fork to cut the butter into the flour until the mixture resembles coarse crumbs.
9. Gradually add the ice water, a tablespoon at a time, and mix until a dough forms. You may not need to use all of the water.
10. Roll out the dough on a floured surface to fit the size of your baking dish.
11. Pour the filling into a greased baking dish.
12. Place the rolled-out crust over the filling, trimming any excess dough and crimping the edges.
13. Cut a few slits in the crust to allow steam to escape.
14. Bake in the preheated oven for 30-35 minutes, or until the crust is golden brown and the filling is bubbly.
15. Remove from the oven and let the vegan pot pie cool for a few minutes before serving.

Enjoy your delicious and comforting vegan pot pie!

Vegan coconut curry

Ingredients:

- 1 tablespoon coconut oil or vegetable oil
- 1 onion, diced
- 3 cloves garlic, minced
- 1 tablespoon grated fresh ginger
- 1 bell pepper, sliced
- 2 carrots, sliced
- 1 small eggplant, diced
- 1 cup diced potatoes
- 1 cup diced tomatoes (fresh or canned)
- 1 can (14 oz) coconut milk
- 2 tablespoons Thai red curry paste
- 1 tablespoon soy sauce or tamari
- 1 tablespoon maple syrup or brown sugar
- Juice of 1 lime
- Salt and pepper to taste
- Fresh cilantro, chopped, for garnish (optional)
- Cooked rice or noodles, for serving

Instructions:

1. Heat the coconut oil or vegetable oil in a large skillet or pot over medium heat.
2. Add the diced onion to the skillet and cook until softened, about 5 minutes.
3. Add the minced garlic and grated ginger to the skillet and cook for another minute until fragrant.
4. Add the sliced bell pepper, sliced carrots, diced eggplant, and diced potatoes to the skillet. Cook, stirring occasionally, for about 5-7 minutes until the vegetables start to soften.
5. Stir in the diced tomatoes, coconut milk, Thai red curry paste, soy sauce or tamari, maple syrup or brown sugar, and lime juice. Season with salt and pepper to taste.
6. Bring the mixture to a simmer, then reduce the heat to low and let it cook for about 15-20 minutes, or until the vegetables are tender and the flavors have melded together.

7. Taste and adjust the seasoning if needed, adding more salt, pepper, or lime juice to taste.
8. Serve the vegan coconut curry hot, garnished with chopped fresh cilantro if desired. Serve over cooked rice or noodles.

Enjoy your delicious and flavorful vegan coconut curry! You can customize it with your favorite vegetables and adjust the spice level to your liking.

Vegan spinach and artichoke dip

Ingredients:

- 1 tablespoon olive oil
- 1 onion, diced
- 2 cloves garlic, minced
- 1 can (14 oz) artichoke hearts, drained and chopped
- 2 cups fresh spinach, chopped
- 1 (8 oz) package vegan cream cheese
- 1/2 cup vegan mayonnaise
- 1/4 cup nutritional yeast
- 1/4 cup unsweetened non-dairy milk (such as almond milk or soy milk)
- 1 tablespoon lemon juice
- 1/2 teaspoon garlic powder
- Salt and pepper to taste
- Optional: Vegan cheese shreds for topping

Instructions:

1. Preheat your oven to 350°F (175°C).
2. Heat the olive oil in a skillet over medium heat. Add the diced onion and cook until softened, about 5 minutes.
3. Add the minced garlic to the skillet and cook for another minute until fragrant.
4. Add the chopped artichoke hearts to the skillet and cook for 2-3 minutes.
5. Stir in the chopped spinach and cook until wilted, about 2-3 minutes.
6. In a large mixing bowl, combine the cooked onion, garlic, artichoke hearts, and spinach with the vegan cream cheese, vegan mayonnaise, nutritional yeast, non-dairy milk, lemon juice, garlic powder, salt, and pepper. Mix until well combined.
7. Transfer the mixture to a baking dish and spread it out evenly.
8. If desired, sprinkle vegan cheese shreds over the top of the dip.
9. Bake in the preheated oven for 20-25 minutes, or until the dip is heated through and bubbly.
10. Remove from the oven and let the dip cool for a few minutes before serving.
11. Serve the vegan spinach and artichoke dip warm with tortilla chips, crackers, sliced baguette, or fresh vegetable sticks for dipping.

Enjoy your delicious and creamy vegan spinach and artichoke dip! It's sure to be a hit at your next party or gathering.

Vegan stuffed cabbage rolls

Ingredients:

For the cabbage rolls:

- 1 large head of cabbage
- 1 cup cooked rice (white or brown)
- 1 can (15 oz) lentils, drained and rinsed (or cooked lentils)
- 1 onion, finely chopped
- 2 cloves garlic, minced
- 1 carrot, grated
- 1/4 cup chopped fresh parsley
- 1 teaspoon dried thyme
- Salt and pepper to taste

For the tomato sauce:

- 1 can (14 oz) diced tomatoes
- 1 can (6 oz) tomato paste
- 1 cup vegetable broth
- 2 cloves garlic, minced
- 1 teaspoon dried basil
- 1 teaspoon dried oregano
- Salt and pepper to taste

Instructions:

1. Preheat your oven to 375°F (190°C). Grease a large baking dish with olive oil or cooking spray.
2. Bring a large pot of water to a boil. Carefully remove the core from the head of cabbage and place the whole cabbage in the boiling water. Cook for about 5 minutes, or until the outer leaves are softened and easy to peel off. Use tongs to carefully remove the cabbage from the water and set it aside to cool.

3. In a large mixing bowl, combine the cooked rice, lentils, finely chopped onion, minced garlic, grated carrot, chopped fresh parsley, dried thyme, salt, and pepper. Mix until well combined.
4. Once the cabbage is cool enough to handle, carefully peel off the softened outer leaves, being careful not to tear them. Place the leaves on a clean work surface.
5. Place a spoonful of the rice and lentil mixture onto each cabbage leaf, near the stem end. Roll up the leaf, tucking in the sides as you go, to form a tight roll. Place the cabbage rolls seam side down in the prepared baking dish.
6. To make the tomato sauce, in a medium mixing bowl, combine the diced tomatoes, tomato paste, vegetable broth, minced garlic, dried basil, dried oregano, salt, and pepper. Stir until well combined.
7. Pour the tomato sauce over the cabbage rolls in the baking dish, covering them evenly.
8. Cover the baking dish with aluminum foil and bake in the preheated oven for 45-50 minutes, or until the cabbage rolls are tender and cooked through.
9. Remove the foil and bake for an additional 10-15 minutes, or until the sauce is bubbly and slightly thickened.
10. Serve the vegan stuffed cabbage rolls hot, garnished with additional chopped parsley if desired.

Enjoy your delicious and comforting vegan stuffed cabbage rolls! They're perfect for a hearty dinner any day of the week.

Vegan falafel

Ingredients:

- 1 can (15 oz) chickpeas, drained and rinsed
- 1/2 cup fresh parsley, chopped
- 1/2 cup fresh cilantro, chopped
- 1/4 cup diced onion
- 2 cloves garlic, minced
- 2 tablespoons all-purpose flour (or chickpea flour for gluten-free)
- 1 teaspoon ground cumin
- 1 teaspoon ground coriander
- 1/2 teaspoon baking powder
- Salt and pepper to taste
- Olive oil, for frying

Instructions:

1. In a food processor, combine the drained and rinsed chickpeas, chopped parsley, chopped cilantro, diced onion, minced garlic, flour, ground cumin, ground coriander, baking powder, salt, and pepper. Pulse until the mixture is well combined and forms a coarse paste. You may need to scrape down the sides of the food processor bowl a few times.
2. Transfer the falafel mixture to a bowl and refrigerate for at least 30 minutes to allow it to firm up.
3. After chilling, remove the falafel mixture from the refrigerator. Using your hands, shape the mixture into small balls or patties, about 1-2 inches in diameter.
4. In a large skillet, heat enough olive oil to cover the bottom of the skillet over medium heat.
5. Carefully place the formed falafel balls or patties into the hot oil, working in batches if necessary to avoid overcrowding the skillet. Cook for 3-4 minutes on each side, or until golden brown and crispy.
6. Once cooked, transfer the falafel to a plate lined with paper towels to drain any excess oil.
7. Serve the vegan falafel hot, as desired. You can enjoy them in wraps, sandwiches, salads, or as part of a mezze platter with hummus, tahini sauce, and fresh vegetables.

8. Store any leftover falafel in an airtight container in the refrigerator for up to 3-4 days. Reheat them in a toaster oven or skillet until warmed through before serving.

Enjoy your delicious homemade vegan falafel!

Vegan mushroom gravy

Ingredients:

- 2 tablespoons olive oil or vegan butter
- 1 onion, finely chopped
- 2 cloves garlic, minced
- 8 oz (225g) mushrooms, sliced (such as cremini or button mushrooms)
- 2 tablespoons all-purpose flour (or gluten-free flour blend)
- 2 cups vegetable broth
- 1 tablespoon soy sauce or tamari
- 1 teaspoon Worcestershire sauce (make sure it's vegan)
- 1/2 teaspoon dried thyme
- Salt and pepper to taste

Instructions:

1. Heat the olive oil or vegan butter in a skillet over medium heat. Add the finely chopped onion and cook until softened, about 5 minutes.
2. Add the minced garlic to the skillet and cook for another minute until fragrant.
3. Add the sliced mushrooms to the skillet and cook, stirring occasionally, until they release their moisture and start to brown, about 5-7 minutes.
4. Sprinkle the flour over the mushrooms in the skillet and stir to coat evenly. Cook for another minute to toast the flour slightly.
5. Gradually pour in the vegetable broth, stirring constantly to prevent lumps from forming. Bring the mixture to a simmer.
6. Stir in the soy sauce or tamari, Worcestershire sauce, dried thyme, salt, and pepper. Simmer the gravy for 5-7 minutes, or until it thickens to your desired consistency, stirring occasionally.
7. Taste and adjust the seasoning if needed, adding more salt and pepper to taste.
8. Once the gravy has thickened, remove it from the heat.
9. If desired, you can blend the gravy with an immersion blender or transfer it to a blender to achieve a smoother consistency.
10. Serve the vegan mushroom gravy hot, ladled over mashed potatoes, roasted vegetables, or vegan meatloaf.

Enjoy your delicious and flavorful vegan mushroom gravy! It's perfect for holiday dinners or any time you're craving a comforting and savory sauce.

Vegan risotto

Ingredients:

- 1 tablespoon olive oil
- 1 onion, finely chopped
- 2 cloves garlic, minced
- 1 cup Arborio rice
- 1/2 cup dry white wine (optional)
- 4 cups vegetable broth, warmed
- 1 cup mushrooms, sliced
- 1 cup fresh spinach, chopped
- 1/2 cup nutritional yeast (for cheesy flavor, optional)
- Salt and pepper to taste
- Fresh parsley, chopped, for garnish (optional)
- Vegan Parmesan cheese, for serving (optional)

Instructions:

1. In a large skillet or saucepan, heat the olive oil over medium heat. Add the finely chopped onion and cook until softened, about 5 minutes.
2. Add the minced garlic to the skillet and cook for another minute until fragrant.
3. Add the Arborio rice to the skillet and cook, stirring constantly, for 1-2 minutes until the rice is lightly toasted.
4. If using, pour in the dry white wine and stir until it's mostly absorbed by the rice.
5. Begin adding the warm vegetable broth to the skillet, about 1/2 cup at a time, stirring frequently. Allow each addition of broth to be mostly absorbed by the rice before adding more. Continue this process until the rice is cooked through and creamy, about 20-25 minutes. You may not need to use all of the broth.
6. While the risotto is cooking, in a separate skillet, sauté the sliced mushrooms until they release their moisture and start to brown, about 5-7 minutes. Add the chopped spinach to the skillet and cook until wilted. Set aside.
7. Once the risotto is creamy and cooked to your liking, stir in the cooked mushrooms and spinach mixture.
8. If using, stir in the nutritional yeast for a cheesy flavor. Season the risotto with salt and pepper to taste.

9. Remove the risotto from the heat and let it sit for a few minutes to thicken slightly.
10. Serve the vegan risotto hot, garnished with chopped fresh parsley and vegan Parmesan cheese if desired.

Enjoy your delicious and creamy vegan risotto as a comforting main dish or side!

Vegan broccoli cheddar soup

Ingredients:

- 2 tablespoons olive oil
- 1 onion, diced
- 2 cloves garlic, minced
- 3 cups broccoli florets
- 3 cups vegetable broth
- 1 cup unsweetened non-dairy milk (such as almond milk or soy milk)
- 1/4 cup nutritional yeast
- 1/4 cup all-purpose flour (or gluten-free flour blend)
- 1 cup vegan cheddar cheese, shredded
- Salt and pepper to taste

Instructions:

1. In a large pot, heat the olive oil over medium heat. Add the diced onion and minced garlic, and cook until softened, about 5 minutes.
2. Add the broccoli florets to the pot and cook for another 5 minutes, stirring occasionally.
3. Pour in the vegetable broth and bring the mixture to a simmer. Let it cook for about 10-15 minutes, or until the broccoli is tender.
4. In a small bowl, whisk together the non-dairy milk and flour until smooth. Slowly pour the mixture into the pot, stirring constantly, to thicken the soup.
5. Stir in the nutritional yeast until well combined. Allow the soup to simmer for another 5 minutes, stirring occasionally.
6. Use an immersion blender to blend the soup until smooth and creamy. Alternatively, you can transfer the soup to a blender and blend in batches until smooth.
7. Once the soup is blended, return it to the pot over low heat. Stir in the shredded vegan cheddar cheese until melted and well incorporated.
8. Season the soup with salt and pepper to taste.
9. Serve the vegan broccoli cheddar soup hot, garnished with additional shredded vegan cheddar cheese if desired.

Enjoy your delicious and creamy vegan broccoli cheddar soup! It's perfect for a comforting meal on a chilly day.

Vegan quiche

Ingredients:

For the crust:

- 1 1/4 cups all-purpose flour (or whole wheat flour for a healthier option)
- 1/4 teaspoon salt
- 1/2 cup vegan butter, cold and cubed
- 3-4 tablespoons ice water

For the filling:

- 1 block (14 oz) extra-firm tofu, drained and pressed
- 1 tablespoon olive oil
- 1 onion, diced
- 2 cloves garlic, minced
- 2 cups chopped vegetables (such as spinach, bell peppers, mushrooms, broccoli, etc.)
- 1/4 cup nutritional yeast
- 1/2 teaspoon turmeric (for color)
- 1 teaspoon dried thyme
- Salt and pepper to taste

Instructions:

1. Preheat your oven to 375°F (190°C).
2. To make the crust, in a food processor, combine the all-purpose flour and salt. Add the cubed vegan butter and pulse until the mixture resembles coarse crumbs.
3. Gradually add the ice water, 1 tablespoon at a time, and pulse until the dough comes together and forms a ball. Be careful not to overmix.
4. Transfer the dough to a lightly floured surface and roll it out into a circle large enough to fit your pie dish. Carefully transfer the dough to the pie dish and press it into the bottom and sides. Trim any excess dough and crimp the edges. Prick

the bottom of the crust with a fork to prevent air bubbles from forming. Place the crust in the refrigerator while you prepare the filling.
5. To make the filling, crumble the drained and pressed tofu into a bowl and set aside.
6. In a skillet, heat the olive oil over medium heat. Add the diced onion and cook until softened, about 5 minutes. Add the minced garlic and cook for another minute until fragrant.
7. Add the chopped vegetables to the skillet and cook until tender, about 5-7 minutes. Season with salt and pepper to taste.
8. Transfer the cooked vegetables to the bowl with the crumbled tofu. Add the nutritional yeast, turmeric, dried thyme, salt, and pepper. Stir until well combined.
9. Remove the pie crust from the refrigerator and spoon the tofu and vegetable mixture into the crust, spreading it out evenly.
10. Bake the quiche in the preheated oven for 35-40 minutes, or until the crust is golden brown and the filling is set.
11. Allow the quiche to cool for a few minutes before slicing and serving.

Enjoy your delicious and flavorful vegan quiche! You can serve it warm or at room temperature, with a side salad or roasted vegetables for a complete meal.

Vegan tofu scramble

Ingredients:

- 1 block (14 oz) extra-firm tofu, drained
- 2 tablespoons olive oil
- 1 onion, diced
- 2 cloves garlic, minced
- 1 bell pepper, diced
- 1 cup diced tomatoes (fresh or canned)
- 2 cups fresh spinach, chopped
- 2 tablespoons nutritional yeast
- 1 teaspoon ground turmeric
- 1/2 teaspoon ground cumin
- 1/2 teaspoon paprika
- Salt and pepper to taste
- Optional toppings: avocado slices, chopped fresh cilantro, sliced green onions, hot sauce

Instructions:

1. Use your hands or a fork to crumble the tofu into small pieces, resembling scrambled eggs. Set aside.
2. In a large skillet, heat the olive oil over medium heat. Add the diced onion and cook until softened, about 5 minutes.
3. Add the minced garlic to the skillet and cook for another minute until fragrant.
4. Add the diced bell pepper to the skillet and cook for 3-4 minutes until slightly softened.
5. Stir in the diced tomatoes and cook for another 2-3 minutes until heated through.
6. Add the crumbled tofu to the skillet, along with the nutritional yeast, ground turmeric, ground cumin, paprika, salt, and pepper. Stir well to combine.
7. Cook the tofu scramble, stirring occasionally, for 5-7 minutes until the tofu is heated through and lightly browned.
8. Stir in the chopped fresh spinach and cook for another 2-3 minutes until wilted.
9. Taste and adjust the seasoning if needed, adding more salt, pepper, or spices to taste.
10. Once the tofu scramble is cooked to your liking, remove it from the heat.

11. Serve the vegan tofu scramble hot, garnished with your favorite toppings such as avocado slices, chopped fresh cilantro, sliced green onions, or hot sauce.

Enjoy your delicious and satisfying vegan tofu scramble! It's perfect on its own or served with toast, potatoes, or a side of fresh fruit.

Vegan cashew cheese sauce

Ingredients:

- 1 cup raw cashews, soaked in water for at least 4 hours or overnight
- 1 cup unsweetened non-dairy milk (such as almond milk or soy milk)
- 1/4 cup nutritional yeast
- 2 tablespoons lemon juice
- 2 cloves garlic, minced
- 1 teaspoon onion powder
- 1/2 teaspoon mustard powder
- 1/2 teaspoon smoked paprika
- Salt and pepper to taste

Instructions:

1. Drain and rinse the soaked cashews and place them in a blender or food processor.
2. Add the non-dairy milk, nutritional yeast, lemon juice, minced garlic, onion powder, mustard powder, smoked paprika, salt, and pepper to the blender.
3. Blend the ingredients until smooth and creamy, scraping down the sides of the blender as needed. If the sauce is too thick, you can add more non-dairy milk, a tablespoon at a time, until you reach your desired consistency.
4. Taste the cashew cheese sauce and adjust the seasoning if needed, adding more salt, pepper, or lemon juice to taste.
5. Once the sauce is smooth and creamy and seasoned to your liking, transfer it to a saucepan.
6. Heat the sauce over medium-low heat, stirring constantly, until warmed through. Be careful not to let it boil.
7. Once warmed, remove the sauce from the heat and serve immediately.
8. You can drizzle the vegan cashew cheese sauce over pasta, vegetables, or use it as a dip for chips or crackers. Enjoy!

Note: Leftover cashew cheese sauce can be stored in an airtight container in the refrigerator for up to 4-5 days. Reheat it gently on the stove or in the microwave before serving.

Vegan mushroom bourguignon

Ingredients:

- 2 tablespoons olive oil
- 1 onion, diced
- 2 cloves garlic, minced
- 2 carrots, diced
- 2 celery stalks, diced
- 8 oz (225g) mushrooms, sliced (such as cremini or button mushrooms)
- 1 cup pearl onions, peeled
- 2 tablespoons tomato paste
- 2 cups vegetable broth
- 1 cup red wine (use a vegan variety)
- 2 bay leaves
- 1 teaspoon dried thyme
- Salt and pepper to taste
- Fresh parsley, chopped, for garnish (optional)

Instructions:

1. Heat the olive oil in a large pot or Dutch oven over medium heat. Add the diced onion and cook until softened, about 5 minutes.
2. Add the minced garlic to the pot and cook for another minute until fragrant.
3. Add the diced carrots and diced celery to the pot and cook for another 5 minutes until they start to soften.
4. Stir in the sliced mushrooms and pearl onions, and cook for another 5 minutes until the mushrooms start to release their moisture.
5. Add the tomato paste to the pot and stir to coat the vegetables.
6. Pour in the vegetable broth and red wine, and add the bay leaves and dried thyme. Stir to combine.
7. Bring the mixture to a simmer, then reduce the heat to low. Cover the pot and let it simmer gently for about 30 minutes, stirring occasionally, until the vegetables are tender and the flavors have melded together.
8. Taste and season the mushroom bourguignon with salt and pepper to taste.
9. Once the bourguignon is cooked and the sauce has thickened slightly, remove the bay leaves from the pot.

10. Serve the vegan mushroom bourguignon hot, garnished with chopped fresh parsley if desired.
11. Enjoy your delicious and comforting vegan mushroom bourguignon! It's perfect served over mashed potatoes, pasta, or crusty bread.

Vegan pumpkin soup

Ingredients:

- 1 tablespoon olive oil
- 1 onion, diced
- 2 cloves garlic, minced
- 1 tablespoon grated fresh ginger
- 4 cups pumpkin puree (you can use canned pumpkin or make your own by roasting and blending fresh pumpkin)
- 3 cups vegetable broth
- 1 can (14 oz) coconut milk
- 1 tablespoon maple syrup or brown sugar
- 1 teaspoon ground cinnamon
- 1/2 teaspoon ground nutmeg
- Salt and pepper to taste
- Optional toppings: toasted pumpkin seeds, coconut cream, fresh herbs

Instructions:

1. In a large pot, heat the olive oil over medium heat. Add the diced onion and cook until softened, about 5 minutes.
2. Add the minced garlic and grated fresh ginger to the pot, and cook for another minute until fragrant.
3. Stir in the pumpkin puree, vegetable broth, coconut milk, maple syrup or brown sugar, ground cinnamon, and ground nutmeg. Season with salt and pepper to taste.
4. Bring the soup to a simmer, then reduce the heat to low. Let the soup cook, uncovered, for about 15-20 minutes, stirring occasionally, to allow the flavors to meld together.
5. Once the soup is heated through and the flavors have developed, remove it from the heat.
6. Use an immersion blender to blend the soup until smooth and creamy. Alternatively, you can transfer the soup to a blender and blend in batches until smooth.
7. Taste the soup and adjust the seasoning if needed, adding more salt, pepper, or spices to taste.

8. Serve the vegan pumpkin soup hot, garnished with your favorite toppings such as toasted pumpkin seeds, a drizzle of coconut cream, or fresh herbs.
9. Enjoy your delicious and creamy vegan pumpkin soup as a comforting meal or appetizer! It pairs perfectly with crusty bread or a salad for a complete meal.

Vegan tempeh bacon

Ingredients:

- 1 block (8 oz) tempeh
- 2 tablespoons soy sauce or tamari
- 1 tablespoon maple syrup
- 1 tablespoon apple cider vinegar
- 1 tablespoon olive oil
- 1 teaspoon smoked paprika
- 1/2 teaspoon garlic powder
- 1/2 teaspoon onion powder
- 1/4 teaspoon ground black pepper
- Optional: Liquid smoke for extra smoky flavor

Instructions:

1. Slice the tempeh into thin strips, about 1/4 inch thick.
2. In a shallow dish or bowl, whisk together the soy sauce or tamari, maple syrup, apple cider vinegar, olive oil, smoked paprika, garlic powder, onion powder, black pepper, and optional liquid smoke.
3. Place the tempeh strips in the marinade, making sure they are well coated. Let the tempeh marinate for at least 30 minutes, or up to overnight in the refrigerator for maximum flavor.
4. Preheat your oven to 375°F (190°C). Line a baking sheet with parchment paper or lightly grease it with oil.
5. Arrange the marinated tempeh strips in a single layer on the prepared baking sheet.
6. Bake the tempeh bacon in the preheated oven for 15-20 minutes, flipping halfway through, until the strips are crispy and browned to your liking.
7. Once the tempeh bacon is cooked, remove it from the oven and let it cool for a few minutes before serving.
8. Serve the vegan tempeh bacon hot as a side dish, crumble it over salads or sandwiches, or use it as a topping for vegan burgers or pizzas.
9. Enjoy your delicious and savory vegan tempeh bacon! It's perfect for adding a smoky flavor to all your favorite dishes.

Vegan chocolate avocado mousse

Ingredients:

- 2 ripe avocados
- 1/4 cup cocoa powder
- 1/4 cup maple syrup or agave syrup
- 1 teaspoon vanilla extract
- Pinch of salt
- Optional toppings: fresh berries, shredded coconut, chopped nuts

Instructions:

1. Cut the avocados in half, remove the pits, and scoop out the flesh into a food processor or blender.
2. Add the cocoa powder, maple syrup or agave syrup, vanilla extract, and a pinch of salt to the food processor or blender.
3. Blend the ingredients until smooth and creamy, scraping down the sides of the bowl or blender as needed to ensure everything is well combined.
4. Taste the mousse and adjust the sweetness if needed by adding more maple syrup or agave syrup, a tablespoon at a time.
5. Once the mousse is smooth and creamy and sweetened to your liking, transfer it to serving bowls or glasses.
6. Cover the bowls or glasses with plastic wrap and refrigerate the mousse for at least 1 hour to chill and firm up.
7. Serve the vegan chocolate avocado mousse chilled, topped with your favorite toppings such as fresh berries, shredded coconut, or chopped nuts.
8. Enjoy your delicious and healthy vegan dessert! It's perfect for satisfying your chocolate cravings while also providing a dose of healthy fats and nutrients from the avocado.